THE CELL BLOCK PRESENTS…

SUCCESS UNIVERSITY

MIKE ENEMIGO & JOSHUA KRUGER

Published by: The Cell Block™

The Cell Block
P.O. Box 1025
Rancho Cordova, CA 95741

Website: thecellblock.net
Facebook/thecellblock.net
Instagram: @mikeenemigo
Corrlinks: info@thecellblock.net

Copyright © 2021, by Joshua Kruger

Cover Design: Mike Enemigo

Send comments, reviews, interview and business inquiries to: info@thecellblock.net

All rights reserved. This book may not be reproduced in whole or in part without written permission from the publisher, except by a reviewer who may quote brief passages in a review; nor may any part of this book be reproduced, stored in retrieval system, or transmitted in any form or by any means, electronic, mechanical, photocopying, recording, or other, without written permission from the publisher.

WARNING DISCLAIMER

This book is designed to provide helpful and informative material on prosperity, building a better life, and achieving your dreams. It contains the opinions and ideas of its author. It is sold with the understanding that the reader requires personal assistance or advice, a competent professional should be consulted.

It is not the purpose of this book to require every tip, tactic, and/or strategy that is available to a prisoner for achieving prosperity, but instead to compliment, amplify, and supplement other books. You are urged to read all the available information and material, including the books listed throughout this work, learn as much as you can, and then develop your own strategies and work your own plan.

Having true prosperity is not some pie-in-the-sky get-rich-quick scheme. Anyone who wishes to achieve success must decide to invest a lot of time and effort into it. The advice and strategies contained in this book may not be suitable for every situation. The purpose of this book is to educate and entertain. However, there will probably be errors, both typographical and in content. Because of this, it should be used as a guide, and not the be-all, end-all book on prosperity and success for prisoners. The fact that a website, business, organization, and/or association is listed or referred to in this book as a citation and/or a potential source of further information does not mean the author or publisher endorses the website, business, organization, and/or Association, or what those entities may offer. It should also be noted that the Internet websites listed, and other entities referred to, may have, by the time you are reading this warning, changed, disappeared, closed and or dissolved.

Some terms mentioned in this book are known to be or are suspected of being trademarks of different entities. Use of a term in this book should not be regarded as affecting the validity of any trademark or service mark.

The author and publisher specifically disclaim any responsibility for any liability, loss, or risk, personal or otherwise, which is included as a consequence, directly or indirectly, of the use and application of any of the contents of this book.

Praise for *The Millionaire Prisoner* Books

On *The Millionaire Prisoner:*

"I'm so impressed by Josh's work, I felt compelled to write and say I believe this book will help thousands of prisoners focus on a more positive and profitable life. I have seen a lot of submission for publication, but Josh's is by far, the best I've seen."
– George Kayer, CEO of *Girls and Mags*; original editor of *Inmate Shopper*

"*The Millionaire Prisoner* is a terrific guidebook for prisoners who desire to make something more of their life, even while in custody."
– Christopher Zoukis, author of *College For Convicts* and *Federal Prison Handbook*; founder of www.prisonlawblog.com & www.prisoneducation.com.

"The Millionaire Prisoner is one of the best books a prisoner can read. From A-Z, this book is the ultimate blueprint for how to hustle and win legally, from your prison cell, turn your negative into a positive and get REAL money. If you read and implement the information in this book, you are guaranteed prosperity. It's a must have in every prisoner's collection."
– Mike Enemigo, author, CEO of The Cell Block & Self-made Millionaire Prisoner

"I absolutely love your book . . . My mom paid $20 for it. It's definitely worth it."
– Jonathan R., Texas Prisoner

"... *The Millionaire Prisoner* is a must-read for all prison entrepreneurs. The information/perspective it gives is unique and motivating."
– King Guru, author of *How To Write Urban Books For Money & Fame, Prisoner Edition*

"It is like a breath of fresh air to be working on a manuscript that is so positive and helpful to people who are in need of that kind of support. You will most surely be an inspiration to many who read your book. Your words have helped me also as I type."
– Jane Eichwald, *Ambler Document Processing*

"*The Millionaire Prisoner* is a mandatory must-have book for any prisoner that is tired of just going through the motions in prison. *The Millionaire Prisoner* honestly changed my way of thinking. If you're tired of asking your family and friends for money and want to make your own, get this book and learn how to become a Millionaire Prisoner."
– Joshua "Butterbean" Snyder, IL. Prisoner

"... Your book is like the gospel to all prisoners and go-getters. I ordered your book *The Millionaire Prisoner* and I love it because it's full of wisdom, can put money in my pocket and gives us lessons based on morals – integrity – and principles that will set the stage for success with no limits!"
– Jewell Saunders, Missouri prisoner

"Two thumbs up for this book. One would have to be a complete fool not to take advantage of the program that is shared in *The Millionaire Prisoner*."
– Jeremy Winsor, IL. Prisoner

"I am so grateful that I had the opportunity to read The Millionaire Prisoner ... it was the sole inspiration when I first

started this mail order company. Your wisdom and example have helped me grow into my potential. I would not be where I am today without the knowledge you shared in your teachings."
— Steven Ortiz Soto, *Ortiz Publishing Group*

"Thank you for writing *The Millionaire Prisoner*. For me, this book will be one book that I will never throw away."
— Donnell Harrison, NY. Prisoner

On *Celebrity Female Star Power*:

"Josh Kruger has done it again. Other companies may offer lists but nothing like the thousands of addresses in this book. This book is worth hundreds of dollars!! The price alone makes this book a steal. If you like celebs like I do, this book is a MUST have for you too."
— A. Meyer, Illinois prisoner

On *PenPal Success*:

"In a nutshell, armed with the knowledge of my results thus far:
Would I buy *PenPal Success* again? For sure.
Was it worth the money? Absolutely.
Did I benefit from it? Without a doubt.
Thanks to your publication I have met some really great people from around the world. And my life is enriched because of it."
— Russell H., federal prisoner

"Wow! You didn't leave anything out, a masterful presentation and tutorial on pen palling."
— George Kayer, CEO of *Girls and Mags*

"I'm pleased to say that your system does work, one gal has fallen madly in love with me."
– John H. Akron OH.

"Read *PenPal Success*. It can show you how."
– Krista Smith, author of *Pen Pals: A Personal Guide for Prisoners*

"You're a genius. I just came off a visit with my girl. Your book works! Thanks bro."
– C.B., Illinois prisoner

INTRODUCTION

"A journey of a thousand miles begins with a single step."
– Lao Tzu

In prison, anyone can be anything they want. Most of us prisoners have built-in bullshit detectors that we've honed over our lifetime. I've spent over 27 years of my life incarcerated and I've heard all kinds of game that prisoners run. One of the biggest areas of prison life where you can't really fake stuff is the size of your bank account. If you got money you can live like a King inside prison. If you got money you go to commissary regularly, have magazine subscriptions, use the phone (maybe you have your own phone?), and order all the packages you can. Of course, money isn't everything, but it certainly helps your incarceration go smoother. Because of this, I've made it my business to find prisoners who were making money legally while inside. Then I try to use what they are doing in my own life so I can make my prison stay better, easier, and less harsh. Sometimes it works for me, sometimes it doesn't. Writing books works for me. I started writing books because I saw other prisoners doing it and making money. This will be my fifth book in seven years. In research for my books, I found many prisoners who were making things happen. Some of you may know some of these prisoners from my articles in *Inmate Shopper*, or my books, *The Millionaire Prisoner*™ and *Cellpreneur*™? I tell my story in all my books which I'll now share briefly for those of you who haven't read it, or heard it before.

> *"An expert is a person who has made all the mistakes that can be made in a very narrow field."*
> – Niels Bohr

Who I Am and My Role in Your Life

I'm a 42-year-old author serving a life sentence for felony murder conviction. I started doing time when I was 14. On this bid I have been down since 1999. I used to be in a gang in a small town in central Illinois. I sold drugs and did armed robberies. I was dumb as hell. Even though my family lived in Section 8 housing and got food stamps so we could eat, I still had every opportunity to go down a different path. I had a job offer to work at UPS. I was in Community College to become an architect. I also had a good paying job at a major distribution center in the Midwest. But I couldn't stay the course and the streets kept calling me. So, I wound up back in jail fighting the death penalty. While in the County jail my baby mama gave birth to beautiful twin girls and it was then that I had to change my life. At the subsequent bench trial in 2000, I received a direct verdict of acquittal when the State of Illinois refused to participate over an evidence dispute. I was released, but eventually rearrested after the state successfully got the Not Guilty verdict vacated on appeal. See People V. Kruger, 327 Ill. App. 3d 839, 764 N.E.2d 138 (4th Dist. Ill. 2002). At the 2003 jury trial, I was acquitted on intentional murder, but convicted of felony murder and sentenced to life in prison without parole. See People V. Kruger, 363 Ill. App. 3d 1113, 845 N,E, 2d 96 (4th Dist. Ill. 2006).

After reading several of Zig Ziglar's books, I reached out to the late, great motivational speaker and began corresponding with Ziglar. I adopted Zig's philosophy that you can have everything you want in life if you just help enough people get what they want. Tired of depending on friends and family for support, I signed up for, and graduated from, Crown Financial Ministries. I decided to leverage my extensive juvenile and adult prison experiences into a freelance writing career. In 2011, I launched my micropublishing empire from my prison cell by self-publishing two booklets, *How To Get Free Pen-Pals* and *How To Win Your Football Pool*. Prison authorities seized my property and threw me in segregation by alleging that I was violating prison rules. Not to be dismayed, I kept going and published my first book, *The Millionaire Prisoner*™. It took me only 30 days to write my second book, *Pen Pal Success*, which is based on my personal experiences from behind the iron veil of prison. After the success of both of these books a lot of prisoners started asking me how I did it. So, I wrote my third book, *Cellpreneur: The Millionaire Prisoner's Guidebook*, to show prisoners how to legally start a business from their prison cell.

For the past 15 years I've been obsessed with finding strategies that prisoners can use to better their lives. I've wrote about a lot of them in my books. Becoming an author has helped me in all areas of my life. It has certainly helped me financially. But the thing I love most is when I get letters from other prisoners thanking me for writing the books that I have. That's worth more to me than all the royalty checks I've ever got. Yet still, I've always known that there were people (including prisoners) who were making a whole lot more money than me. One of those prisoners was Mike Enemigo, the CEO of [The Cell Block](#)™, and self-made Millionaire Prisoner™. He reached out to me about doing some stuff together and I said yes. The reason I said yes is because game recognized game and I saw another cellpreneur who was making things happen. Here's what Mike says about making things happen:

"Despite being sentence Life Without Parole to prison in 2002, I stay trying to make something happen; whatever it may be. I've never been one to let things – even prison walls, steel bars and razor wire – stop me from doing what I set out to do. And in order to be successful, I've had to build up a network of relationships and resources. After all, especially when trying to accomplish something from inside a prison cell, where you're forced to rely on assistance from other people on the outside, it is all about networking, relationships, and resources.

During the time I've spent doing the various things that I do and gathering up the much-needed resources, I learned that there are actually a lot of things prisoners have available to them and can do, that most just don't know about. But with the proper information, some creativity (you *must* learn to think outside of the box when you live in one) and determination, there are many, *many* things that can be done. And yes, you can do them right from the inside of *your* prison cell, too..."

That's what this book is about. To teach you some strategies that will help you achieve all of your dreams in life. Both Mike and I are lifers. He in Cali, me and Illinois. He got sentence in 2002, me in 2003. You can say that we were on a crash course, and it was inevitable that we put our minds together to produce products and services that can help you. That's our mission in a nutshell: to deliver quality information to your cell that you can use right away to make things happen. No fluff, no filler. Just straight game laced by two cellpreneurs who are living out what we preach and teach. We invite you to "come get some". We know that you won't be disappointed.

How This Book Was Written

This book is a collaboration between both me and Mike. A few years ago, IDOC confiscated all of the typewriters in the maximum-security prisons. I haven't let that stop me from writing. What I did was write out this book in longhand with little 3-inch flexible ink pens. Then I sent my handwritten manuscript pages to Mike who would edit them and type them up. He'd add his little changes or put in additional insights from his prison experiences. So even though this book sounds like it was mostly written by me (Josh), it's the work of both of us. And we hope to continue to bring you additional books in *The Millionaire Prisoner*™ lineup.

How to Get Your Money's Worth from This Book

Read it, peruse it, study it. Master it. But the only way the knowledge in this book can become wisdom is if you implement it into your life. To help you do this I came up with a simple formula for reading and studying how-to information that can help you master it. (I had the help of my mentor, the late, great motivational speaker and author, Zig Ziglar, in coming up with this formula.) Here's how you can read this book to get the most from it:

1. Read through this book quickly to get the gist of the message, underlining or highlighting the things that really "grab" you. Only stop to look up words you don't know, or write them down to look up later. This first reading allows you to become familiar with the book.

2. As you read this book the second time, keep a notebook of ideas generated by the book that you can personally use. The objective is not to see how quickly you can get out of the book, but what you can get out of the book.

3. In your third reading, invest time and patience in gleaning additional ideas you may be missing in your second reading. Carefully examine each chapter. Go over what you have highlighted or underlined. Put anything you missed in your notebook.

4. The fourth reading will enable the book to become an integral part of you, enhancing your effectiveness. After this reading, you can place the book in your collection, and it will be a treasure trove, ready and willing to supply you with any knowledge you may need.

5. Find other prisoners who have read this book, or share it with them, and then discuss it together to see what you got out of it. You may gain additional insights from their ideas and thoughts that you didn't see on your own.

A Few Final Words

We invite you to stay in touch with us. The tips, tactics, in strategies that I advocate using in this book will need to be updated as better processes become available. I intend to learn those new processes and use them... and share them with you. If you find some success systems that a prisoner can use, or if you experience success using their boat, right and let me know about it. There is a questionnaire in the back of this book that we hope you fill out and return to us. I just might put you in the next edition of this book or other

Millionaire Prisoner™ products. Also, so that we can congratulate you, not just for what you achieved, but for making the world a better place by beginning to break the cycle of prison. Let's get to it. You can start by turning the page and taking a step forward on your Millionaire Prisoner™ journey.

CHAPTER ONE

Your Basic Foundation

"A successful man is one who can lay a firm foundation with the bricks others have thrown at him."
– David Brinkley

The firm foundation of a cellpreneur is a great attitude. *The Millionaire Prisoner*™ attitude is one of no fear, no guilt, and no excuses. It's one of determination, dedication, and discipline. It's one that requires a belief that prison doesn't stop shit. The first chapter in *The Millionaire Prisoner: Part 1* is all about how you can acquire the proper mind frame. But I want to briefly assist you in case that you haven't had the chance to read my first book yet? If at the end of this chapter you're still having trouble believing that anything is possible, then I encourage you to get a copy of *The Millionaire Prisoner: Part 1*, and study it.

Your attitude is comprised of what you believe, what you speak, what you do, and how you act. A "millionaire prisoner" attitude is one that's congruent with that of a millionaire. *TMP* Cellpreneurs speak different, act different, and do different things than the average prisoner. Most of you have probably heard a few prisoners say they are "a convict, not an inmate." I used to say that as well, but didn't really understand the difference. What is it? Their attitude towards prison life. Now I don't even say that. Instead, I say, "I'm a cellpreneur, a millionaire prisoner." This requires a totally different attitude. And to actually become a self-made millionaire prisoner requires a radically different attitude altogether. I'll use Mike Enemigo and I as examples.

We think different than most prisoners. Almost prisoners are thinking about some hot chick they want to bang, or their next drug scheme, or both? We're thinking about how to make millions of dollars from our prison cells. For us, it's "M.O.B." like 2PAC rapped a long time ago. Of course, we like, and appreciate, beautiful women. Except we believe it's far more important for us to secure our financial future first. (BTW, if you become a self-made millionaire prisoner, you'll have plenty of opportunities to bag that beautiful woman you want!)

If you could spend the day in the cell with either Mike or me, I'm sure you would understand that we act different. Most of my cellmates have hated being in the cell with me. Why? Because I don't play cards, chess, or any other games while in my cell. I don't sit around and trade war stories. I'm not mean to my cellies. I just understand that my time is valuable. Right now, as I write this my television is turned off. I'm sitting at my desk writing. My cell is my office. Yes, it also happens to be my kitchen, bathroom, and bedroom. But for the majority of the time, it's my office. This is not to say but I don't watch TV or play games. I do both. I watch sports or a movie on my downtime. I'll play games when I'm on the yard. I'll show you in a later chapter how to maximize the use of your time for the best results. For now, you must think like a Millionaire Prisoner™ and or Cellpreneur™. That begins with behaving in sync with your new positive attitude.

THE MILLIONAIRE PRISONER: PART 3

> *"You don't get what you (inherently) deserve. You get what you deliberately and intentionally attract, not only by who you are, but also by what you think, say, do, and get others to do. By the situations, circumstances, contacts, relationships, and opportunities you engineer."*
> – Dan S. Kennedy, marketing guru, author of the *NO B.S.* book series, and self-made multimillionaire

As you start forming this Millionaire Prisoner attitude your fellow prisoners will try to make you feel guilty about it. They will say you changed because you don't waste time like they do anymore. You'll need to develop some thick skin and learn how to go against the grain. Trust me though, once you start achieving success, they'll come to you with their hands out asking for stuff. Don't let them guilt-trip you. Get it all out of your head right now. Wealth is unlimited. So is money. They print more and more of it every week at the U.S. Mint. There's plenty for you to get, me to get, Mike to get, and your fellow prisoners to get. There should be no guilt in your mind about this fact. Nor should you have any guilt about being a Cellpreneur on your Millionaire Prisoner journey. Don't allow someone else to put that idea into your mind either!

You also shouldn't have any fear. Scared money makes no money. This is the easiest part for me. I came from nothing. My family was poor. We got food stamps and lived in an old roach-infested house in the ghetto. So, I had to steal and sell drugs to make money. Of course, that led me to prison. Once I began this cellpreneurial journey I had no fear about failure. I was used to having nothing in my past. So if

I went back to that it would be nothing different because I survived it once. But if I just achieved a little bit of success, it would be such a win that I didn't think of any type of fear. You're in prison already, so what do you have to fear? Nothing. You have everything to gain.

In *The Millionaire Prisoner: Part 1* I wrote about Ryan Blair. He grew up with an abusive father, had to sleep in a lice-infested shack, and was put on medication for ADD and depression. He joined a gang and wound up in juvenile prison. But that didn't stop him. He formed a great attitude, reprogrammed his mind and became a multimillionaire CEO. He wrote a book with the perfect title, *Nothing To Lose, Everything To GAIN*. You can do it also. Remember to have no fear, because you have nothing to lose, but everything to gain!

The biggest excuse that I hear from the prisoners I talk to is that they "can't" do something because they are in prison. But prison doesn't stop shit! Mike and I are living proof that a wall, or fence topped with razor wire doesn't stop you from achieving your dreams. We are self-made Millionaire Prisoners who did it all *after* we got sentenced to life in prison. We didn't do it in the free world. We don't have a computer in our cell with Internet access. Yet none of those facts have stopped us. I have been placed in segregation for "running a business." My books have been placed on the banned book list at some Illinois prisons. I have been threatened by staff because of my book writing. So, what did it stop? Nothing. I won't let it, or them, stop me from achieving my dreams. Prison, and all that comes with it, is just an obstacle that I must go through, around, and over, to achieve my goals. Excuses are the bricks that make the house of failure. While your fellow prisoners make the excuse that they can't do something because of the fact that they are in

THE MILLIONAIRE PRISONER: PART 3

prison, you won't. Now you believe that anything is possible. How do you know this? Because there are many real-life cellpreneur examples to choose from.

Here are a few.

Robert Beck, using the pen name Iceberg Slim, wrote his first book, *Pimp: The Story of My Life*, while in jail. Charles, "Roc" Dutton is also a former prisoner. While inside, Roc started a prison drama club and got his GED. Upon leaving prison he went to college. He's now an actor, whose credits include his own Fox TV series, *Roc*, and movies like *A Time To Kill* and *Legion*. Danny Trejo may be the most famous former prisoner turned actor. While inside California prisons he got his high school diploma and became the welterweight boxing champion of San Quentin. Now you can see him everywhere and in tons of movies and TV shows. From now on, every time, you see him on your TV screen you can think that he was once where you're at. Get your attitude right and you could be where he's at?

There are plenty of other examples out there. When you have a cellpreneurial mindset you'll start to see them everywhere. In the March/April 2020 *Inc.* magazine Dennis Hunter was profiled. Hunter was developing therapeutic cannabidiol (CBD) and running his own marijuana growing business in 1998. Then the FBI raided his spot and he lost 12,480 cannabis plants and spent six years in prison. After his release he founded CannCraft in 2014, which will legally produce 146,000 pounds of cannabis and hemp. CBD was legalized in 2018 and it's estimated that it will become a $16 billion industry by 2025. In 2019, Hunter's company had $46 million in sales! He didn't let prison stop him and neither should you.

A lot of musicians have spent time in prison before getting out and succeeding in the music game. Maino did 10 years in prison for a drug-related kidnapping conviction. His face bears the scar from a razor fight while inside. After he got out he met DJ Kay Slay and then dropped his album, *If Tomorrow Comes* . . . He ended up getting a shoe deal with Fila. He's just one of many who have used music to make money after prison.

Shawn Hartwell got sentenced to 20 years in prison at the age of 18 for being a drug kingpin as a member of the "E'Port Posse" in New Jersey. They were profiled in *DonDiva* magazine. After he got out he became the #1 celebrity promoter in New Jersey and started a successful branding company and podcast. He's been seen in a lot of magazines like *Kite* and *Straight Stuntin*. The main thing that allowed him to succeed was his attitude. Going to prison didn't stop shit!

Marcus Bullock did seven years in prison for carjacking. He got out and started Flickshop.com. They allow free-world people to convert social media snapshots into postcards mailed into prisons. His company was profiled in the *Washington Post* and *Forbes* magazine. He hires ex-offenders and visits prison to teach business skills.

Formal federal prisoner Vincent Bragg cofounded ConCreates – a marketing agency that crowdsources ideas from prisoners or people affected by the criminal justice system.

Eddie Bunker used his time in California prisons to write books. His memoir *Education of a Felon* made me want to write books. One of his novels was turned into the movie *Straight Time*, starring Dustin Hoffman. After he got out he was cast in the movie "Reservoir Dogs." Hollywood Fame.

THE MILLIONAIRE PRISONER: PART 3

What do all of these examples mean for you? It means that you can do it also. In this book I'll give you some strategies and tactics that successful people have used to achieve their dreams. I'll show you some that I use. I'll show you some that Mike uses. But all of these tactics and knowledge will mean nothing if you don't believe that anything is possible and that prison doesn't stop shit. I'll say that again: PRISON DOESN'T STOP SHIT!

> *"When you get your attitude right, you can handle anything the world throws at you. Even life in prison."*
> – Bill Dallas

No more excuses. No more fear. Believe in yourself. Believe in your dreams. Anything is possible. The rest of this book can help make it more probable.

> *"It is not fate that bars your path. It is not lack of money or opportunity. It is yourself – your attitude towards life. Change it – and you change all."*
> – Robert Collier

CHAPTER TWO

F.O.C.U.S.: Time Revolution for Cellpreneurs

> *"Concentrate all your thoughts upon the work at hand. The sun's rays do not burn until brought to a focus."*
>
> – Alexander Graham Bell

Why time Revolution and not time management? Because you're in prison and your time is already managed for you! You're told when to go to the chow hall to eat. You're told when to go to yard or gym. You're told when to go to the Chapel. You're told when to go to school or work. You're told when to lock up. Even if you're in a minimum-security prison you're still under someone else's time management system. What you need is a time Revolution so you can make time serve you, instead of you serving time. In this chapter I'll show you how.

> *"The first step toward success is taken when you refuse to be a captive of the environment you first find yourself in."*
>
> – Mark Caine

As much as you may dislike President Trump's political views, he has come up with some good business ideas. In one of his books, he has a chapter on "F.O.C.U.S." which stands for "Follow One Course Until Successful." When I first read that I thought it sounded cool. But I didn't really implement it into my life. I still tried to multitask and get everything done all at once. Then I read a book called *The One Thing* by Gary Keller (with Jay Papasan). In that book he also quotes the F.O.C.U.S. principle. And that's when it all clicked for me. It all came back to F.O.C.U.S. if you want to achieve great things.

"The secret of getting ahead is getting started."
– Mark Twain

Anthony Robbins teaches the same thing in his *Time of Your Life* seminar. He calls it the "RPM" method. RPM stands for "Rapid Planning Method". The principle behind it is to ask yourself three questions so you FOCUS on "Results, Purpose, and Massive action." Because what you FOCUS on you will go to. So, the first step to a time Revolution is to find out specifically where you want to go? Or what you want to achieve?

"If you chase two rabbits you will not catch either one."
– Russian Proverb

Because of my books I get a lot of prisoners who come up to me and tell me their ideas. They want to get my opinion. Most of the time I asked them to stop and answer ONE question: "What do you really want?" They normally look at me dumb-faced and say, "I want money." That's not good enough for me so I'll ask them again, "What do you specifically want to achieve?" I'm trying to get them to clarify their goal or objective. Because until they know that specific answer, they can't possibly know the correct road to take. Their idea may be good, but it could be the wrong road for their ultimate objective. You won't know *how* to use your time until you know *where* you're going.

My goal in this chapter is to get you to transform your life by how you treat prison time. A lot of free world people will ask you how you spend your time in prison? Your answer should be, "I'm not spending time or serving time. I'm investing my time so it serves me." The goal is to learn how to use your "free time" to produce something valuable that brings in a measurable return. To do that you're going to have to stop doing some things you're doing right now. Let me give you an example.

From 2002-2008 all I did was spend my in-cell time writing penpals. The reward I sought was weekly visits, phone calls, and the here and there money orders they could (or would) send. Yes, I achieved what I wanted as you know if you've read my book, *Pen Pal Success*. But as I look back on those years, I think about how stupid I was. I wasted 6 years writing every day. Fast forward to 2014. I'm in segregation and spent 30 days working on *Pen Pal Success*. That 30 days of work has produced more results financially than anything else in those six years. Don't get me wrong, those pen pal years were fun and that experience led me to write *Pen Pal Success*. I just wasn't really happy. I wasn't fulfilled. That came after I wrote the books.

"Happiness is not pleasure. Happiness is victory."

THE MILLIONAIRE PRISONER: PART 3

– Anthony Robbins

Because I wasn't accomplishing my objectives in the timeframe that I wanted I realized I had to change it up. So, what did I do? I went on a search to find prisoners who were achieving huge things behind bars. I wanted to read their books to see what they were doing to get their results. I knew it had to be different than what I was doing. Maybe if I stole their daily habits, I could start getting the same kind of results they were getting?

I studied Eddie Bunker and how he wrote his books while in Folsom and other Cali prisons. I studied Danny Trejo, Billy Wayne Sinclair, Paul Wright, Jerry "The Jew" Rosenberg, Malcolm X, and Nelson Mandela. One prisoner that I learned a lot from is Michael Santos. He's free now and a millionaire. I read all of his books. One of his books shows you a typical day inside prison for him. It's called *Prison! My 8,344th Day*, and it's a great exposé on how he used his days to invest into his future.

Here's what he wrote:

> "My objective is to succeed upon release. I don't care about a prison reputation and I'm indifferent to staff perceptions. The pursuit of success upon release drives my everyday decision, and that has been the case since the beginning of my term."

Notice what he said. His "objective" drove "every decision". That was his ONE thing. His FOCUS. He got it.

This is the first step to a time Revolution. Finding out what your ONE thing is. You must ask yourself some questions to clarify your objective. This strategy of finding the where is the key to deciding the tactics to use to get there. Remember this formula: Strategy = the where + tactics = the how to. Strategy is the overall goal and tactics are how you achieve that goal. I'll show you some tactics later. First, we got to find out what your main objective is.

> "When you walk with purpose, you collide with destiny."
> – Bertice Berry

There're two steps to finding out your main objective. Both require you to ask yourself some questions. What do you really want? What specifically do you want? For me, I wanted $6,000 a year or $500 a month. How did I come up with that number? I added up everything I would need to live good in prison (commissary, GTL music subscription, magazine and newspapers, email and phone) and then I divided the costs per month to get my number. I'm doing life in prison so that's all I needed to live rich in here. Once I came up with that number, my next question became: "What's the ONE thing I can do to earn $6,000 a year (or $500 a month) such that by doing it everything else will be easier or unnecessary?" (Thank you, Gary Keller, for teaching that question in *The ONE Thing*.) The answer for me was to create and sell how-to information products.

Can you specifically tell me what you want? Here's an exercise to help you figure it out. Picture your perfect life. What vision comes to mind? What kind of car are you driving? What do you do for a living? What kind of house do you live in? What kind of food are you eating? Do you have any kids? A wife or husband? Own a business? Write your

THE MILLIONAIRE PRISONER: PART 3

answers down. Be specific. My neighbor told me he wants a Lamborghini. OK, I said, "I'll give you a 1985 Lamborghini Countach." No, he didn't want that. He wants a blue Lambo. A new one. So, I told him to write down "I'm driving a blue, 2025 Lamborghini Gallardo." That's specific. Imagine this perfect life. Then write it all down in the present tense like it's happening:

"I'm driving a 20_____."
"I'm living in a _____ in the city of _____."
"I own a _____ and I bring in $_____ a year."
"I have a _____ and we have _____ kids."

These are just some fill-in-the-blank examples. Yours could be different? The key is to find out the answers so you can specifically find out what you need to do to create this perfect dream life? Write it all down now.

> "If you can't explain your goal to a 6-year-old child, you probably aren't clear about it yourself."
> – Albert Einstein

Did you write down all the stuff you really want? If not, go back and do it. If you did it, I want you to look at your list and see how many require money to get? House, car, business, toys are all money goals. So, you can add them all up together and that's your money goal.

Now look at your list and decide which one is the most important to you? Think about the "why" behind it? What emotion does it bring forth? Mine was based on fear. I was scared of living the rest of my life in prison and not having what I needed. My family wouldn't be around forever. A lot of my lifer friends were older and didn't have anybody in the free-world to help them out. I hated that feeling because it scared the shit out of me. I made a decision to never be in that position. Emotion is a powerful incentive. So put the feeling – the why – behind what you want.

Once you have it all down then find the ONE item on the list that if you accomplished it would make all the others easier or unnecessary? Really think about this. Because whatever you select will be your FOCUS.

Now that you know what your goal is – the where you want to be – you need a map to get there. The first step to creating your map is to use the 80/20 rule.

The 80/20 Principle is a book by Richard Koch based on the Pareto Principle. What it demonstrates is that 80% of the results you achieve come from 20% of the actions you take. Richard Koch grew $4 million in 1990 into $230 million in 2014 using the 80/20 principle to invest in companies. Wouldn't you like to get those same type of results in your own life? I would. We can start by using the 80/20 principle to evaluate our time. If 20% of the actions you take produce 80% results you get, that means 80% of the actions you take produce 20% of the results you get. Put another way. If you wrote 10 letters this week, 2 of them would get you what you wanted and the other 8 might not do diddly squat. The key is to find out what works and do more of that and stop doing what doesn't work.

> *"If you pay attention to the wrong thing you could waste your entire life polishing turds."*
> – Perry Marshall

THE MILLIONAIRE PRISONER: PART 3

Based on this principle I'm going to give you some guidelines to use to come up with the tactics you'll use daily that will help you achieve whatever you want. These are based on my personal experiences and the studies I did of other successful prisoners.

> *"Focus is a matter of deciding what things you're not going to do."*
> – John Carmack

- Before you read anything ask yourself, "will I need this information for something immediate and important?" If not, don't read it.
- Don't mistake busyness for business. Cleaning your cell and doing laundry will not help you achieve your goals. Michael Santos paid another prisoner to do it for him so he could use his time for more important things.
- It's not the quantity of your work that matters, but the quality. No multitasking. Focus and work on one task until it's done.
- No news radio or talk radio while you're working on your ONE thing. Music? Yes, if there's no talk in between songs. No television, except a maximum of two hours a night. (This means one game or one movie only!)

> *"Poor people have big TV's. Rich people have big libraries."*
> – Jim Rohn

- Be prepared for delays or lockdowns on movement. Do something productive while you wait.

- Choose your allies carefully. Because you're a sum of the five people who you spend the most time with. You also need people who respect you enough to leave you alone while you work.

> *"Surround yourself only with people who are going to lift you higher."*
> – Oprah Winfrey

- Find unconventional ways to invest your time. It may require you to go the opposite of your prison peers. For me, it meant skipping yard to work on a book chapter.
- Don't let people steal your time with dumb questions or idle chatter. I put headphones on and ignore everybody when I'm writing.
- Don't try to cram everything into one hour. Take breaks. Studies show that short (1/2 hour) bursts of work with breaks after that produce more quality.
- Bundle tasks together. Clean cell/wash clothes. Answer mail/email. Read magazines/newspapers.
- Exercise, even if it's just a brisk walk for 15 minutes in the morning. It's good for your body and energy levels. Also, eat right.

> *"People do not decide their futures, they decide their habits and their habits decide their futures."*
> – E.M. Alexander

Here's the most important tactic in this chapter. Find a time block of four hours a day where you can work on your ONE thing. You want this to be at high energy time for you. And you need it to be the time where you will have no distractions. Michael Santos got up early in the morning so he would have the study room all to himself. Eddie Bunker stayed up late into the night when his prison was quiet. I do the same thing. When can you do it? Find it, then schedule it daily.

> *"One hour per day of study will put you at the top of your field within three years. Within five years you'll be a national authority. In seven years, you can be one of the best people in the world at what you do."*
> – Earl Nightingale

After you have found your time block that will allow you to work uninterrupted for four hours you need to list what you will do during that time block. The key is to do a daily "To Do List" the night before. What is your ONE thing? What do you have to do daily to get there? Schedule that first every day. Say you want to write a book. Schedule to write a page a day at first. Then two pages a day. Then four. Michael Santos did 4 pages a day, or 25 pages a week. That's good. With that you'll have a complete rough draft in two months. The key is to schedule your To Do List the night before and then reviews it once you get up in the morning.

> *"When you create a list of everything you have to do the next day, your subconscious mind will then work on that list all night long while you sleep. Often you'll wake up in the morning with ideas and insights on how to do the job better and in less time."*
> – Brian Tracy

Use the time when you first get into your four-hour time block as creative time. Or "maker time." Use the rest of your day for the trivial and mundane. Or "manager time." Invest those four hours every day by studying and creating. Think about leverage. Ask yourself, "Is what I'm doing to get my ONE thing anywhere close to the highest and best approach out there?" If not, stop doing it and go do the best thing.

> "Anything that isn't relevant, that you're not competent in, or that you're not completely passionate about should be delegated to somebody else."
>
> – Jay Abraham

If you can find the ONE thing that you can FOCUS on daily and you have a purpose behind it you can get it. Write out your MAP and your daily To Do List and then work every day at the same time on that To Do List and you'll become the most productive prisoner at your prison.

If you want more strategies and tactics for your time Revolution I highly recommend three books:

- *NO B.S. Time Management for Entrepreneurs* by Dan S. Kennedy
- *Master Your Time, Master Your Life* by Brian Tracy
- *The ONE Thing* by Gary Keller

> "There is no 'how.' Just do it."
>
> – Bruce Lee

21 Things To Remember Each Day As You Start Your Day

THE MILLIONAIRE PRISONER: PART 3

1. No one can ruin your day without your permission.
2. Most people will be about as happy as they decide to be.
3. Others can stop you temporarily, but you can do it permanently.
4. Whatever you are willing to put up with is exactly what you will have.
5. Success stops when you do.
6. When your ship comes in, make sure you're willing to unload it.
7. You will never "have it all together."
8. Life is a journey . . . not a destination. Enjoy the trip!
9. The biggest lie on the planet: "When I get what I want, I'll be happy."
10. The best way to escape your challenge is to overcome it.
11. I've learned that, ultimately, "takers" lose and "givers" win.
12. Life's precious moments don't have value unless they are shared.
13. If you don't start, it's certain that you won't arrive.
14. We often fear the thing we want the most.
15. He or she who laughs . . . lasts.
16. Yesterday was the deadline for all complaints.
17. Look for opportunities . . . not guarantees.
18. Life is what's coming . . . not what was.
19. Success is getting up one more time.
20. Now is the most interesting time of all.
21. When things go wrong, don't go with them.

CHAPTER THREE

3 Ways to Use Your Tablet for Succe$$
"The successful person has developed the habit of doing the things failures don't like to do."
— Albert E.N. Gray

At the end of the movie "Inside Man" (starring Clive Owen and Denzel Washington), Owen's character has locked himself in a makeshift cell for a week behind a fake wall in the banks' storage room. He says that just because you're in a cell doesn't mean you have to be in prison. How true. (By the way, it's a great movie and if you haven't seen it, you should watch it.)

Success from prison starts with the right mindset. It's why I started both this book, and *The Millionaire Prisoner*, with chapters about "attitude." You must have the right mental attitude. You get it by realizing that even though you're in prison your mind is free. Or it can be and should be! In this chapter I'll show you how to use a MP3 player or tablet to help free your mind and get the right attitude.

A lot of prisons and jails allow us to purchase tablets. Some prisons give them out free. The version that I have, and use, is a GTL INSPIRE™ tablet. Yours may be different, but the strategy will be the same. You can do two things with your tablet. The first is you can listen to music and play games all day. That's what most prisoners do. That's fine if

THE MILLIONAIRE PRISONER: PART 3

you are already a millionaire. Are you? If not, then you need a different strategy. Your life won't change until you do something different in your life. Prison is a negative place. The whole mentality is one of lack. Of pain. Of past mistakes. You have to guard your mind from this negativity. Some of us have to reprogram our minds. I did. You start this process by changing your state. That leads me to the second way you can use your tablet. You can use it to free your mind and body. That in return, will help you achieve your dreams.

3 Ways To Use Your Tablet For Success

Successful prisoners use their tablets when they exercise, when they read and write, and when they're sleeping. Let me explain. The easiest way to change your state is to get up and move around. When you wake up in the morning don't lay around in bed. Get up and do something. Make your bed. Put on your shoes. Exercise. Write something. Do anything. Here's what I do. I get up, make my bed, wash up and brush my teeth. These things tell my body that I'm up for the day. Then I turn on my tablet and listen to it while I exercise. OK, I'm getting a little ahead of myself. It wasn't always like this.

When I first got my tablet, I just listened to all the songs I had never heard from my favorite artists. Then my wife told me I needed to get back on the grind. And Mike told me I needed to catch my second wind and start writing again. They were right. I needed more energy. I knew I could use my tablet to do it also. Costas Karageorghis, Ph.D, is head of sport, health, and exercise sciences at Brunel University in London, and author of *Applying Music in Exercise and Sport*.

He told *Cosmopolitan* magazine in 2018 that music can make some exercises seem about 10% easier and boost your mood 15%. I needed a boost in my mood because I was in burnout mode.

Then I read an article by Tim Ferriss (*The Four-Hour Workweek, Tools for Titans* author) where he gave an exact exercise formula and how to use music for better performance. Here's the exercise formula with actual songs:

> WARM UP: 90 – 115 beats per minute (bpm)
> [use 2 or 3 songs in a row]
> "Express Yourself" by Labrinth (94 bpm)
> "Feels" by Calvin Harris, Pharrell (101 bpm)
> WORK OUT: 120 – 136 bpm
> "We R Who We R" by Ke$ha (120 bpm)
> "Lose Control" by Missy Elliott (125 bpm)
> "I like It" by Cardi B (136 bpm)
> COOL DOWN: 120 – 136 bpm
> "My House" by Florida (94 bpm)
> "Ferrari" by Bebe Rexha (77 bpm)

Those songs came from author Leslie Goldman. You don't have to use those exact same songs. I just wanted you to see the formula that can make your workout seem easier and lift your spirits. That's one way you can use the tablet.

The second way is to use it as a motivational tool. One day I was playing around on my tablet and ran a search for my mentor Zig Ziglar. For those of you who have read my first book, *The Millionaire Prisoner*, you know that Zig was very influential in the beginning of my cellpreneurial journey. He passed away a few years ago, but his legacy lives on. The search for his name brought up some speeches and programs he had on the tablet. I listened to them and they helped me get inspired and back into the Millionaire Prisoner mindset. So, I started doing searches for all of my mentors. Anthony Robbins, Chris Widener, Earl Nightingale, and Napoleon Hill all came up. There are other classic talks and books on the tablet as well. I like to listen to them when I watch football or basketball. You can do the same.

Some of my favorite speeches to listen to are those from Motiversity. My favorite are those by Walter Bond. He's a former NBA player and his speech I like best is "*Shark Mindset 2*". I have a shark tattooed on my arm and I identify with the shark as my spirit animal. Ever since I read Harvey Mackay's great book, *Swim with the Sharks Without Being Eaten Alive*, I have tried to keep moving like a shark. Sometimes I falter and need a push forward or pick me up. Listening to Walter Bond's motivational speeches help me change my state and get ready to tackle the day. Are you getting up to thrive? To seize the day? A shark is constantly on the hunt. Are you? I know it sounds like some hocus pocus stuff, but listening to these talks can aid you on your journey.

When I write articles or work on my books I like to listen to music. I have ADD and music helps me tune out the daily prison noise and focus on my writing. Some of my favorite songs are *Lose Yourself* by Eminem, *Hall of Fame* by The Script, and *I Just Want to Be Successful* by Drake. Stephen King listens to hard rock while writing his horror novels. What can you listen to? Here's something I learned from millionaire author and investor, Tim Ferriss (*The 4Hour Workweek; The 4Hour Body;* and *Tools for Titans*): Listen to the same playlist over and over again. One, it allows you to just write and not worry about messing around with the tablet. Two, it does something to your mind and allows you to get into a zone. Ferriss explains the science of it better than me in his books. I just know it works. You want to listen to music that motivates you. Or that moves you. If I'm writing an article about getting money, I like to listen to songs that talk about hustling or getting money. Like PayRoll Giovanni's albums, including *10 Stack Commandments*. Or Lil Baby's Song, *Get Money*. It may take you a few hours to put these different playlists together, but it will be worth it. No matter what you're working on there's something on the tablet that could aid and assist you on your journey to the top.

For more information on how music can help you, be sure to check out the book, *Your Playlist Can Change Your Life* by Galina Mindlin, Don Durousseau, and Joseph Cardillo.

The last strategy is to use your tablet for better sleep and self-help hypnosis. Pick a time when you won't be bothered by staff or other prisoners. Then tune into a program or talk that is dealing with the problem you want to work on, or the spot where you want an edge. Type in "subliminal hypnosis" into your tablet and watch all the stuff that pops up. Pick the ones you're interest in and listen to them.

When I was a kid my mother used to listen to nature sounds to help her sleep better. Her favorites were those of dolphins, whales, and rainforests. I know some other prisoners who do the same thing. There are plenty of deep sleep meditation talks and sounds on the tablet. You can use them for better sleep. It's best to get quality sleep rather than oversleep. Just search for "deep sleep" on your tablet and try out different ones to see which ones you like best and work for you.

THE MILLIONAIRE PRISONER: PART 3

A successful prisoner will do what an unsuccessful prisoner won't do. Instead of using your tablet to listen to music and play games all day, use it as an educational tool and an entertainment outlet all at the same time. For those of you wondering why I haven't mentioned using the tablet as a communication tool? I will get to that in the networking chapter. Before I leave this topic, I want to give you some of my favorite motivational things to listen to off my tablet. After I wrote this chapter as an article for the 2020-2021 *Inmate Shopper*, GTL redid the whole music streaming process. After I did some searches, I found even more educational and self-help audio tools. Some of my favorite ones were lost also. To help you in your search, here are some names or courses to look up:

Eddie Truck Gordon
Chris Traina
William Hollis
Marko Halilovic
PT Barnum
J. Earl Shoaff
Warren Buffett
Ernest Holmes
Dr. Joseph Murphy
Roger Hamilton
Trent Shelton
Sun-Tzu
Niccolò Machiavelli
Nathan Harmon
John Kremer
Peter Daniels
Olumide Emmanuel
Jim Pancero
Betterlife_Subliminals
Brainwave Mind Voyages
Andrew Johnson

The Honest Guys
Natural Hypnosis
Ashok K. Jain
Frederick Winters
Subliminal Research Group
Terry Elston
Tina Brown
Jairus L. Adams Sr.
Charlie "Tremendous" Jones
Jim Rohn
Time & Life Building Blocks
Troy Coulon (& Troy Coolon)
Steve Luckenbach
Learntoberich.com
David D. Holland
Fearless Motivation
Dr. Dave Williams
Mikael Olsson
Dale Carnegie

Freddy Fri
John C. Bogle
Self Help Institute
REI Club
John Templeton
Self Help Audio Center
Tommy Orlando
Conrad Hilton
Clay Nelson
How to Make Money in Real Estate
Get Results
Business Success Institute
Online Marketing Institute
Pete Williams
Online Business Guide
Small Business Big Money
Selling On eBay
Quit Your Job Guide
Business Success Guide
Learn It!
Best Way To Learn
Lifeline Audio Books
Jeremy Lopez
Real Estate Investing for Beginners
Online Auction Secrets
David Hooper
Bart Milatz
Business Success System
Paul Taylor
Imogene Walker
Personal Success Secrets
Stock Market Success System
Stock Market Guide
Small Business Legal Guide
Productivity Secrets
Earl Nightingale
Unlimited Success Principles
Auction Success System
The Law and Secrets of Success
Personal Finance Guide

Abdel Russell
Career Success Secrets
Better Memory Institute
Healthy Living Institute
Meet New People Daily
Natalie Oman
Genevieve Behrend
Greg Mason
Goal Achievement Institute
Time Management Institute
Be A Magnet to Money
Writer's Guild
Anthony Robbins
Scott Chou
R.H. Jarret

THE MILLIONAIRE PRISONER: PART 3

*In the future we hope to get some Millionaire Prisoner™ audio stuff on your tablet. Keep your eye out for that.

"Self-talk is reinforcing, and people stay stuck in whatever self-talk they've been embracing. Telling yourself your own sad story may be comforting, but it keeps you in prison."

– Perry Marshall

Don't forget to listen to the podcasts on your tablet if you got that app. There're all kinds of great business podcasts out there. Even prison and criminal justice podcasts. This is an untapped goldmine you can dig into.

And last, a lot of tablet providers provide free eBooks on their platform. Most of these eBooks are from books that are in the public domain and free to use for whatever you want. So, use them to better your life. Become a Millionaire Prisoner.

CHAPTER FOUR

Your Network Is Your Net worth

"In poverty and other misfortunes of life, true friends are a sure refuge."

– Aristotle

Multi-millionaire real estate investor and bestselling author, Robert Allen, says that "your income is the average income of your ten best friends."

Business consultant and millionaire author, Brian Tracy, says that "the people you choose to work with or for, to socialize with, or marry, to invest through or go into business with, will determine about 85 percent of your success and happiness in your personal life." He offers a simple equation: QR x QR=PS. What that means is that the quality of your relationship's times the quality of those relationships equals your personal success. How true.

My own experiences in life bear this out. When I was selling drugs and robbing people, most of my friends had been to prison or jail. I ended up in jail also. Now I'm doing life in prison. Once I started reaching out to millionaire authors and entrepreneurs my life started to change. In this chapter I'll show you some of the networking secrets I've learned over the years.

THE MILLIONAIRE PRISONER: PART 3

In his fantastic book, *The Sticking Point Solution*, marketing consultant Jay Abraham says that we need to create a worldwide personal network of quality business players. He wrote that you need three types of people in your network:

1. People who either have the *answers* you need or can connect you with the ones who do.
2. People who have the *resources* you need
3. People who can perform *specialized* tasks far better than you or anyone on your staff.

If you're trying to accomplish anything from a prison cell, you need these people on your team. You can build this network by using technology and a simple letter writing system. Let me explain.

The World is Flat

Technology has leveled the playing field. We no longer play on a little scale. If we want to, we can play in a global arena by using email and the internet. A great book to read about this is *The World is Flat* by Thomas Friedman. Another resource that coincides with this is *Abundance: The Future is Better Than You Think by* Peter Diamonds and Steven Kotter. For those of you who don't have access to the internet you can get over this hurdle by using outside help. My fellow self-made Millionaire Prisoner™ found his website guy in Pakistan. Proof that the world really is flat.

A lot of companies sell services to prisoners offering email, Facebook, Instagram, and Twitter profiles, and internet research. If you don't have someone in your existing network to help you with this you'll have to use one of these companies. My favorite, and the only prisoner assistant company that I endorse, is Help From Outside. I know the owner, and I used to have an account with HFO. If you're serious about success from prison and don't want to depend on family or friends for help, I highly recommend HFO. Send a SASE to:

> Help From Outside
> 2620 Bellevue Way NE #200
> Bellevue, WA 98004
>
> (206) 486-6042
> www.HelpFromOutside.com
> info@helpfromoutside.com

Be forewarned those services start at $30 an hour and a $200 minimum deposit is required to open an account. If you got the money, it is worth it. No matter what you choose to do, you need access to email.

Your Outside Connection – Email

Some of you now have access to email at your prison through JPay, GTL, or Corrlinks. If you do, utilize it when building your network. But don't be fooled, these prison-based email providers are severely limited. I use www.connectnetwork.com via my GTL tablet. Yet, I still can't email anybody I want. They have to log in and sign up to send/receive emails from me. Of course, every email we send is monitored by the prison. For the business-minded prisoner

THE MILLIONAIRE PRISONER: PART 3

you need a regular email account that free-world people can reach you at. I use Google's Gmail system. But you can use other ones like Yahoo or Hotmail. Here are some tips to remember when setting up your email account:

1. Have a great email address. Most people use their name or something catchy like that is significant for them. Don't use goofy email addresses like thugpassion@gmail.com or golddigger@hotmail.com. Put up a professional front.

2. Set up an email auto response that says: "Sorry, but I'm away from the computer at this time and will get back to you as soon as possible."

3. Be cautious of what you write in your subject line. This line is what people see first and it helps them decide whether to open your email or not. Most email service providers use 25-character subject lines. So, create catchy, short, subject lines that make someone want to open your email.

4. If you're using emails to market your services or products then here are some tips that I learned from marketing expert Maria Yudkin (www.yudkin.com):
   a. Highlight why your email is important;
   b. Don't repeat who you are in the subject box because the "From" box already says that;
   c. Use the word FREE if you're offering something valuable;
   d. Try to create temptation in your 25 characters.

Having an email account will open the door for you. It can increase the mail you get and allow you to contact mentors, businesses, and other people who toss out mail from prisoners, but always check their email box.

Do You Have An Email Signature?

If you have your own free-world email account, then you need on email signature (.sig). An email signature is the line of type at the end of your email message. If you have anything to sell, run a business, or offer some type of service, you need a .sig. People must know who you are, what you do, what you have to offer, and how to contact or find you. Here are a few reasons why you should have a. sig:

- It's free to set up.
- Every time you send an email, it will be attached to it.
- You don't have to retype it over and over
- It's another easy way to market your product or services.

Here's something I learned from my mentor, Peter Bowerman. A lot of people just list who they are and their accomplishments. Better for you would be to make your .sig a call to action. Your whole reason is (or should be) to build your network by getting people to keep in touch with you. So move them to start doing that with a call to action in your .sig. Here's how it could look.

THE MILLIONAIRE PRISONER: PART 3

Do you know anyone that has a loved one in prison? Send them to thecellblock.net to learn more about how they can help turn prison into a stepping-stone to success.

Mike Enemigo
The Cell Block
P.O. Box 1025
Rancho Cordova, CA 95741
Facebook.com/thecellblockofficial

For a complete look at how to use email to achieve success in this world I highly recommend freelance copywriter Robert W. Bly's masterpiece, *The New Email Revolution*.

In his little book, *Simple Secrets to Networking Success: Build A Stellar Network in A Couple Months*, Alex Ivanov lists the steps that he used to build his LinkedIn network to over 4,000 people.

Here they are:
- Create business cards with your picture
- Find events on Meetup
- Practice talking to people
- Stay in touch through LinkedIn
- Build confidence through books and conversations

While those are good tactics for those of you who are going to be released soon, they don't help those of us doing long-term prison sentences. But there are some gems in his strategy and I'll briefly discuss those.

Business Cards. The first letter I ever received that fellow info-cellpreneur Mike Enemigo sent me had a business card in it. I was impressed. Here was another lifer who was using free-world networking tactics. Proof that you can do it also. I like the idea of putting your photo on your business cards. If you're not going to do that, then at least use both sides of the card and make it memorable. Here's what my mentor, Peter Bowerman (www.wellfedwriter.com), says about in his book, *The Well-Fed Self-Publisher: How to Turn One Book Into A Full-Time Living*:

"They're always attention-getters, and they just make sense in this 'business card world' of ours (and they make fine bookmarks, thank you very much...). Call them the 'prevailing standard currency of networking.' It's what everyone's used to. I always give out two to people, so they can share one with someone else."

Everyone always talks about Vistaprint (www.vistaprint.com) when telling us where to get these cards. But shop around. Another good place with low prices and great quality business cards is Overnight Prints (www.overnightprints.com).

Books and Conversations. There are several reasons to read a book. One is to pass time and escape your prison. That's how I used to read books years ago. I read fiction books and would get lost in them. My time flew by. But I wasn't achieving success. The second way you can read a book is for what Mark Victor Hansen (of *Chicken Soup For the Soul*® fame) calls "Reading for Opportunity." You read non-fiction books looking to learn specific facts, tactics and strategies to help you achieve your goals. And you read looking for names and

THE MILLIONAIRE PRISONER: PART 3

companies that you can network with and possibly build a working relationship with. This is how I read books now. And not just books, but also magazines and newspapers. For more, let me explain.

Your Network Dream Contact List

Anytime you see a name of someone you'd like to network with, write it down. You do this so you don't forget it. Also, so you can see how many people there are waiting on you to contact them. This is the format I use:

Name	Business	Expertise
Piper Kerman	Author	"Orange Is The New Black"
Richard Stratton	Author/Director	Expert witness for prison cases
John Legend	Singer	Unlocked Futures

Every time I see someone that is doing anything that helps prisoners, or even comes close to the prison system, I write their name down like those above. The list gets longer and longer each week. I will eventually contact everyone on that list.

I learned this strategy from former prisoner Michael Santos. He was a prisoner who got 45 years in the federal system under the draconian cocaine kingpin laws of the 1980's. He wrote several books while inside, including *Earning Freedom*; *Prison! My 8,344th Day;* and *About Prison*. His book *Success After Prison: How I Built Assets Worth $1,000,000 Within Two Years of Release* is highly recommended for any prisoner that's about to go home. While he was inside, he used to send out a letter to people he didn't know in the hopes of building his network.

Here's what he said about these letters:

> "Over the years I've sent thousands of these kinds of unsolicited letters out. As a prisoner, my life is akin to being adrift at sea. To feed myself, I cast a line. The more lines I cast, the more chances I have of finding food to sustain mean. The letters I write to people I don't know may be discarded by the recipients, but I never stop trying. The success I've had over the years convinces me that the effort and stamp are worth the investment. Every year I've increased the depth and breadth of my support network by sending out such letters."

By his practice he became friends with university professors, journalists, lawyers, and even law enforcement officers in the Justice Department. They all supported his bid to earn an early release. After he got out, he became an adjunct professor and taught a class on prisons and parole at a University in California. That's how he became known as "the Prison Professor." You should check out his work at www.michaelsantos.com.

    I know for a fact that his strategy works because I have used it on my own. I was mentored by the late, great Zig Ziglar through letters all because I wrote him a letter thanking him for writing one of his books. Two of my longest-running pen pals have come from me sending out these unsolicited letters. One is my writing mentor. The other is now my surrogate mom. This is why you write these names down. So, you can contact them. And learn from them.

THE MILLIONAIRE PRISONER: PART 3

"Make your friends your teachers and mingle the pleasures of conversation with the advantages of instruction."

– Baltasar Gracian

Most of the people who you want to contact list their address on their website somewhere. Especially if they run a business or sell products of some kind. Even if they don't you can find their email address. And if you are in need of someone to find the address you could use a service that finds people. Barkan Research does that for $17.95 per person per search. You need to know their first and last names. Their last known address (at least the city and state), their date of birth (or approximate age), and any additional facts, like phone number or relatives' names. They typically do this type of search to find witnesses in court cases and defendants to serve lawsuits on. But you could use it for business purposes.

Here's the address:
    Barkan Research
    P.O. Box 352
    Rapid River, MI 49878

After you find their address you can write them a letter or email. It doesn't have to be an elaborate letter. Here's the format I use:

Letter Requesting A Mentorship

Dear (insert expert's name):

I hope this letter finds you in the best of health and spirits. I just finished reading your book, (insert their book title), and I can honestly say that it has truly opened my eyes. I'm trying to learn more about becoming a success in (insert whatever the subject is), and would like for you to mentor me.

In making this request I would like to know what you've learned over the years, and I'm not out to get what you've learned. I would like to be a protege and not a parasite. I do understand that your time is valuable, so what I propose is sending you a letter here and there with the question that I may have? Then you can answer if you get some free time. If it's more convenient you can respond by emailing me at (put your email address here).

Once again, thank you for writing (insert their book). I really like the part about (insert something you like about their book). It was a great read. You can quote me on that and any promotions that you do. Thank you for taking the time to consider my letter in request. I look forward to hearing from you soon. May you and your work be blessed in all that you do.

Respectfully requested,
(Your Name)
(Your Address)

The key to the strategy is to ask them a question that can't be answered by reading their book. If in response to your question they give you another book title to read, get it and read it. Thank them for it. Build good karma. Successful people value their time. So, it they're taking the time to share with you it means a lot. Show them that you value their time and advice by following their instructions. Here are some more tips.

How to Get the Most Out of a Mentorship

1. Choose the right mentor. If you want to be a writer, don't seek out someone who built motorcycles for a living.
2. Be honest. Seek to understand what your mentor has to offer, and what you hope to gain. Discuss it.
3. Be open minded and humble. Don't allow what you think you know to stop you from learning what you need to know.

Have a hunger for learning. Always ask questions. You want what's in their head, not anything they could hand out.
Having a mentor will save you time and money. They should show you the errors in your ways and help you excel. One day you'll be able to show them how much their help aided you on your journey. That will be the ultimate compliment.

> *"Successful people rely heavily on their mentors. Ordinary people don't."*
> – Robert G. Allen

Prison PenPal Websites

Most prisoners use these websites when trying to build outside contacts. I used them for years and in my book, *PenPal success*, I go in-depth on my experiences. I'm semi-retired now from the prison penpal game, but I still use them to network. Let me show you how.

In 2019 I was writing full-time and not looking for any penpals. One of my friends who had read *PenPal Success* suggested that I go back online. That seed of an idea festered in my mind and I eventually went back on *WriteAPrisoner.com*. I only did it because my friend said she would write the penpals for me. She even wrote the ad for me. Here's the ad text:

> Hi, my name is Josh. My friends describe me as smart, self-motivated, loyal, a good friend, comical at times, polite, generous, kindhearted, and humble.
>
> I really enjoy the arts. I personally am an artist who loves to create with words, or you can simply say I'm an accomplished author and poet. I enjoy other types of art as well, especially music. My taste in music is very diverse and eclectic. I enjoy eating, not so much cooking. Although I can make the best peanut butter and jelly LOL.
>
> While here I plan on getting my education finished. I also plan on continuing to find ways to build a better society with my cellpreneurial skill set. Also, I'm focused on getting back into court to overturn my case or to get an early release date.
>
> I look forward to meeting people from all walks of life. I believe diversity is the color that paints the canvas of one bright, beautiful world. I'm willing to correspond for however short or

however long, as long as we both have a positive impact on each other because I know the power of a smile or a simple hello.

Well, I look forward to hearing from you if you made it this far! Here's to a future filled with a lot of laughs and long, beautiful days and star-filled nights. I hope to see a letter that your hand has graced soon. Until then, may you be blessed! Respect.

Of course, I know you want to know about my results? I got numerous hits. Some I do not write anymore. Some I do. Most of the people who responded to this ad were either artists, or had an interest in art. My best penpal is from Chicago and he does arts and crafts. For my birthday, he sent me two books to help me complete this book. Another response I got was from Rebecca. She's a beautiful 19-year-old college student, who is majoring in Art Therapy. So, the ad worked. I got the responses I should have. But there were some problems also.

First, one girl just wanted to get married so we could go on *Love After Lockup*. And she already had a husband that she was separated from! She lived at home with her mom and didn't have a job. We were not a good fit. Another hit I got was from an accountant in a law firm in New York. I thought he might be someone I could network with? But he only wanted to write emails about his foot fetish. For real, I can't make this stuff up. His fantasy was for him to lay on the ground and for me to walk all over him with my size 13, bare feet. He said he wanted me to go so far as to put my feet over his mouth and nose to suffocate him! I'm straight, that's not my cup of tea. He did say he had other prisoners he emailed. Hey, whatever floats your boat. All of us have certain preferences and I'm not passing judgment on y'all. He just wasn't what I was looking for.

The second problem was that after almost 6 months my profile had only been viewed 1,304 times. That equals out to about 217 views a month. The cost of my ad was $40, and I paid $10 to add another photo. So, for $50 I got 1,304 page views, or about 4¢ a view. To really look at it right, do the math this way. Seven hits (or responses) on a $50 profile equals $7 a hit. To be fair to those numbers, we must look at the statistics and demographics behind the penpal game. I'm a lifer, and it says so on my profile page. That brings my response rate down. If I had an outdate that was only a few years away I would get more hits. The other problem is that we don't know the truth about the 1,304 profile views. Are they 1,304 different people? Or is it one girl who looked at my profile then clicked off of it, only to click back onto it again? Does that count as two views or one view? I don't know. What I do know is that if you can circumvent this search process and clone your perfect penpal your success will increase.

My Facebook Story

After my twin brother got out of the fed joint, he helped me build a Facebook page. I've been locked up since 1999 so I had never used Facebook as it did not exist back then. But 17 years later I was on and popping. He built me a simple page and I would make posts here and there. I was able to reconnect with friends that I went to school with and hadn't seen in years. Some of them didn't even know I was doing life in prison! One of them thought I was living in California. LOL.

THE MILLIONAIRE PRISONER: PART 3

One day I was on the yard and saw an all-white cat sitting on a boulder sunning himself. At my prison, the yard is in the back of our prison and is literally carved out of a hill and the Rock wall. This type of earth is common to one area of our woods – the Shawnee National Forest, and Mississippi River area of Illinois. This formation and the way our prison is carved out of the hillside next to the Mississippi River has earned it the nickname, "The Pit." In between the yard fence and the Rock wall are all these boulders that have fallen onto the ground. So, there was this cute, white cat chilling like he didn't have a care in the world. I happen to love cats. I had an all-black cat named "Cosmic Creepers" (or "CC" for short) when I was a kid. I got him as a kitten and named him after the witches' cat in the Disney movie "Bedknobs and Broomsticks." I had CC for years until he got into a fight with a raccoon and the coon tore half of CC's face off. He looked like "Two-Face" from Batman™ and I wanted to keep him, but my mom and the vet made me put him to sleep. Like I said, I love cats. So, I wrote a Facebook post about the all-white cat sunning himself next to our yard.

Immediately, the women who were friends on my page all liked it. Then I got contacted by Nikki. She was a girl who lived in my neighborhood. Her dad and my mom were good friends. She liked my cat post and we started talking. She started coming to see me every week, putting money on my books, and accepting all my calls. Then I started talking to another girl who was friends with my sister growing up. We talked on the phone every day and had weekly video visits. I was doing so good that some of the prison guards who worked the visiting room asked me what my secret was? I was on top of the world, and it was all because of Facebook.

Eventually my brother and I fell out over some business disagreements and I shut my Facebook page down. OK, that's a lie. He told me since he built it for me, he was shutting it down and I would have to start over. He ended up going back to prison for a string of bank robberies. Even though we weren't talking I didn't want him to go back to prison. I'm sure you're wondering about Nikki and the other girl? Both ended up finding free-world guys and we don't talk anymore. No love lost. I understand it all. I can only imagine what kind of burden it is to be in a relationship with a life-term prisoner like me. I learned a lot. The main thing was that Facebook could deliver better results than any prison pen pal website could.

Social Media Pen Pal Networks

A lot of the prison pen pal companies now I understand that by using their social media pages they can get better results for us prisoners. And better results (or more hits) equal more word-of-mouth marketing for their business. That means more money for them. It's good for everyone involved if they do it right!

Caged Kingdom is a business that charges $14 for a yearlong pen pal profile on their website, www.cagedkingdom.net. They also charge $7 for a Facebook promotion. They guarantee your promotion will reach 200 people. These will be people targeted based on the information provided in your profile application. You may be thinking that 200 people is not much? But remember my writeaprisoner.com story? I paid $50 basically for 1,300 profile views. That same $50 could get me 1,400 targeted profile views with Caged Kingdom. And those people should be more responsive than someone just scanning profiles online. When I saw that, I decided to try their services out. Here's what happened.

Caged Kingdom did a Facebook insights promotion for my profile. It was seen by 213 people, shared by 3 people, and engaged by 13 people. I ended up getting a great pen pal off this promotion. Another girl signed up to email me off this promotion. So, it worked. To show you why I consider it a success I must briefly explain the metrics behind all of this.

Hit Counters & Response Rates

When pen pal websites first started there was a bunch of hoopla about "hit counters." These services will tell you that your page was hit by thousands of people. But that was misleading. Just because someone sees your profile doesn't count as a "hit." A hit is a response. That's the only thing that should matter to you. Your "response rate."

In *Advertising With Small Budgets for Big Results*, Linda Carlson says that banner ads on websites pull at a rate of 0.1 percent. Google Adwords expert Perry Marshall says that a 2% clickthrough rate (CTR) is good. Marketing experts try to break even at a .5% response. Those are some basic numbers to go by. Here's how you do the math.

My 2019 writeaprisoner.com profile got 1,304 views and 7 responses in six months. That is .005%. Not good. Using Linda Carlson's .01% rate I should have got at least 14 responses. I wasn't close to any of the above CTR or marketing numbers. My Caged Kingdom on Facebook got 13 engagements on 213 people. That is .06%! A lot better than any other pen pal website I have been on. Even if we only use the

3 people who shared my Facebook as a response, it's still a 0.014% response rate. A lot better than the .005% my writeaprisoner profile got.

Total Hits / Page Views = Response %

Because I wanted to understand Facebook ads even more, I went to the experts to see if there was some stuff that could help us even more. In the *Ultimate Guide to Facebook Advertising*, Keith Krance does a great job of explaining "engagement":

> "Remember, the objective in these types of ads is not necessarily a conversion or a Click to your website (although it can be as a side benefit). The primary objective here in a page post engagement ad is to *engage*.
>
> In Facebook terms, 'engagement' can include clicking the image, playing the video, igniting the post, sharing the post, clicking the link in the post to your website – any number of actions that increase engagement with your audience."

According to that definition my Facebook promotion was a success. But there's still a problem with the way Caged Kingdom is doing it.

For those people who wanted to write me off this Facebook post they would have to either go to Caged Kingdom's site and pay $2.45 to do it through their app, or they would have to physically do it on their own with pen and paper. That's too much work. It would be better to set up a profile on a service that offers the first contact for free. Like writeaprisoner does. Then do your Facebook promotion. Except when you do your promotion you have a "click to write now" button right next to it. That way if they liked your photo and what you were saying they could click onto that button. Then it would take them straight to the page where they can write you for free. Anything other than something like that and you're just asking for too much.

Here's something you may not know? That same $50 I paid for my writeaprisoner profile could get my post seen by at least 41,000 people, maybe up to 110,000 people! Huge difference, right? You can get that by using Facebook's "Boost" promotion. Of course, to do that you'll have to set up a Facebook page. If you don't, you'll have to use a company like Caged Kingdom or another prisoner service provider. But before you do any of this, you need to know what, and who, you're looking for?

Your Pen Pal Avatar

Do you know who your perfect pen pal is? What magazines do they read? What TV shows do they watch? What philosophes do they have? What beliefs do they have? What fetishes do they have? What hobbies do they have? What websites do they visit? You ask these questions so you can target your perfect pen pals online. You'll get more hits for your money this way.

For instance, here's my perfect pen pal avatar:

"My best pen pal is a single, lonely woman, 30+, who reads *INC.*, *Entrepreneur*, and *Prison*

> *Legal News* (or believes in prisoner rights). She watches *Love After Lockup, Shark Tank, The Profit,* ABC's *For Life*."

If I wanted to do one for college students it would be:

> "My best young pen pal is a college student who is majoring in criminal justice, reads *Prison Legal News*, and watches *Love After Lockup*, ABC's *For Life*, and prison documentaries."

So how would I find these people? By using Facebook and other social media sites. I could start with the following searches:

> "Pages liked by people who like Prison Legal News."
> "Pages liked by people who like ABC's For Life."
> "Pages liked by people who like Love After Lockup."
> "Pages liked by the people who like prison pen pals."
> "Pages liked by people who like prisoner rights"
> "Pages liked by people who like prison reform."

I would like all of those pages also. You can also do searches for "people who like _____" also.

Then I would go to Google and search for "prison pen pal forums" and "prisoner rights forums." You do searches like this and you'll find some websites and network opportunities that you've never heard of. They will be opportunities for you to connect with people who are empathetic to the prisoner's journey. Then you start posting in these forums and networking. One way is to ask a simple thought-provoking question? Then, after they answer, you ask them: "How did you come to that conclusion?" I had a cellmate who used to do this on phone calls to the party line. After getting the girls on the line involved in a discussion, he would send them to his online pen pal page. He came up numerous times like that. You can do the same in these forums.

> *"Friends are like the warm blue seat, they splash laughter into your eyes."*
> – Karen Reynolds

You should be on social media only for two reasons. One is to connect with people you don't know. Two, to market your product or services. That's it, that's all.

Most prisoners won't be able to do this right from a cell. So, hire someone to do it for you. But first, read *No B.S. Social Media Marketing* by Dan S. Kennedy and Kim Walsh-Phillips.

To be fair, I only use Facebook to find groups of people I want to network with. Most of my time should be spent on creating great how-to information products for prisoners.

If you want to know more about how to create ridiculously good content for your customers, readers, and online pages, get *Everybody Writes* by Anne Hanley; and *The Digital Crown: Winning at Content on the Web* by Ahava Leibtag.

10 Rules of Posting on Social Media

Guy Kawasaki is a multi-millionaire, and author of numerous books, including *The Art of Start* and *Enchantment*. In *APE: How to Publish a Book*, he gives his 10 unwritten rules of posting on social media. I've borrowed them and adapted them for our situation:

1. <u>Be brief</u>. Two to three sentences at most.
2. <u>Post publicly</u>. Don't hide your good content. Let everyone read it.
3. <u>Post regularly</u>. Three to five posts per day on each service is the right number.
4. <u>Link to the source</u>. This allows people to learn more and is good online business karma.
5. <u>Give credit</u>. Share people's names that give you great material.
6. <u>Include a photo or a video</u>. Kawasaki calls this the "eye candy" of social media.
7. <u>Use the active voice</u>. Not passive, legal jargon.
8. <u>Add a hashtag</u>. #PrisonLivesMatter!
9. <u>Share when your audience is awake</u>. You can do this by using Hootsuite, Buffer and DoShare.
10. <u>Repeat your tweets</u>. Kawasaki says he shares tweets four times, eight hours apart. He doesn't do it on Facebook because it's not standard practice.

"If you have less money in the bank than you have followers on Instagram, you need to get a new group of friends."
– Billionaire P.A.

Pen Pal Growth Secrets

The goal is to build long-term friendships and relationships that are mutually beneficial to both of you. To do that you

need to constantly evaluate these friendships. When you meet someone new, ask yourself the following questions once a week:
- What could I be doing to make both of us happier?
- What could I do less of to make both of us happier?
- What could I start doing to make both of us happier?
- What could I stop doing to make both of us happier?

Go over them with your friends and loved ones. Listen to their answers carefully. When you're with someone, be with him. On the phone? No distractions. When face to face, use eye contact. Touch them. Don't interrupt them. Listen to them. Pause before replying. Ask for clarification. Then paraphrase it back to them. Finally, my number one role is to get rid of negative people in your life.

Networking with Celebrities

We constantly see it play out on TV. A big-name celebrity likes a cause and it takes off. The founders become famous. Or a celebrity helps a prisoner. Like Kim Kardashian-West did for Alice Johnson. Now every prisoner is writing Kim K trying to get out of prison early. Is that a good idea? Some prisoners say we have nothing to lose. I agree. It's worth a shot. But what about networking with Kim K on social media? Here's what FUBU founder, and *Shark Tank* star Damon John said about it in a March/April 2020 *Inc.* article:

> "Twenty-five percent of the people who follow her love her, 25 percent hate her, the other 50 percent are men who just think she's beautiful.

So, you just went down to 25% of the 100% you're paying for."

His advice is to not go out and pay for a big-name celebrity when you can network with smaller ones much easier. He also shared his rule of three. Add three times the value you extract before you ask for anything in return. He shares three of his friend's tweets before he asks them to do the same. All of this is great advice that should be followed. Check out more in Daymond John's book, *Powershift*.

> *"Favor must become your seed before it can become your harvest."*
> – Dr. Mike Murdock

Just because you're in prison doesn't stop you from reaching out to influential people. Even if you don't need them right now, you may in the future. So, dig your well before you're thirsty. Here's how.

Get your "dream contact list." Pick someone. Do they have a website? A newsletter? A blog? Or a book? Sign up for their newsletter. Order their book and then post a review or testimonial on Amazon. If they blog, comment on their posts. Use their #hashtag. Follow them on their social media pages. If they are involved in any associations or organizations, then join those also. One of the best things I did when I first started my own publishing company was to join the Independent Book Publishers Association (IBPA). When I contacted other successful authors, who were IBPA members I said, "I saw your article in *The Independent*..." and they knew I was a member of the IBPA like them. (*The Independent* is the IBPA's newsletter.) Remember Daymond John's rule of three also.

> *"Friendship is born at the moment when one person says to another: 'What! You too? I thought I was the only one.'"*
> – C.S. Lewis

Naturally, you want to join those associations and organizations that you're interested in. That way you can be genuine. Most successful people can spot phony and fake people. Don't do it.

Additional Resources, Tactics & Tips

I could write a whole book about how to network from a prison cell. But I'm limited to only a chapter so I want to give you some additional resources.

If you have a GTL tablet you can listen to the following for more tips on becoming a better networker:

- *I Hate Networking!* By Will Kintish
- *Successful Business Networking Tips* by Kennedy Imuere
- *Networking* by Jon Robert Quinn

Then every once in a while, search "networking" on your tablet to see what comes up.

Some books that you may want to read are:

- *Your Network Is Your Net Worth* by Porter Gale

- *Dig Your Well Before Your Thirsty* by Harvey Mackay
- *How To Win Friends and Influence People* by Dale Carnegie
- *Networking Smart* by Wayne E. Baker
- *Connected* by Nicholas A Christakis
- *Click: The Magic of Instant Connections* by Ori and Rom Brafman

If you're interested in getting penpals then I highly recommend two books:

- *Pen Pal Success* by Josh Kruger (yes, my book!)
- *Pretty Girls Love Bad Boys* by Mike Enemigo & King Guru

Always remember that it only takes one "yes" to change your life. Buy you'll never get that one "yes" unless you try. So, get out of your comfort zone. Write those letters. Send the emails. Build your social media networks. Do whatever it takes. You can start by liking thecellblock.net content online!

CHAPTER FIVE
Money Math
"Even if you trade golden handcuffs for platinum handcuffs, you're still locked up."
— Robert G. Allen

It wouldn't be a Millionaire Prisoner book without talking about money. I've waited till now to discuss money because I wanted to lay a firm foundation first. You needed to get the right attitude, set your goals, and start networking. Now you can begin to go get some money. Because if used right, it has the ability to change your life.

> *"Money doesn't make you different. It makes yure circumstances different."*
> — Malcolm Forbes

I once read a quote by famous lawyer Johnnie Cochran in which he said, "money will determine whether the accused goes to prison or walks out of the courtroom a free man." That has certainly been true for a bunch of celebrities. How many of us would have beat our case if we would have had the money to hire the best criminal defense lawyers? But then again, if we had money in the first place, we wouldn't be doing crime trying to get it! That's what I try to do in my books. Show you a different way to live so in the long run you don't have to live in prison. In this chapter I'll show you how Millionaire Prisoners think about money. You may steal any of the ideas you read in this book. Please use them to build a better life for you and your family.

What is Money?

It's a tool that must be used to have value. You could have a million stuffed near mattress and you'd still be broke. Why? Because it won't do you any good in your mattress. It needs to be invested, or used for your benefit. Money can give you leverage if you know what you're doing. Here's a story of another prisoner that illustrates this.

One of my friends in here won a lawsuit. He used the money to get all of his toys; i.e., tablet, 15-inch TV, fan, razor, shoes, Dickie's coat and a box full of commentary. Nothing wrong with that. I have all of that also. He has about $4,000 left. What's he doing with it? Nothing. For the past three years it has set in his prison trust fund account where it doesn't get interest. He doesn't spend it which is good. He lives off income from his kitchen job. But his $4,000 is not making any money for him. I cringed when I found this out. He doesn't trust someone else in the free world to help grow it so his money doesn't grow. Having lots of money in your prison trust account doesn't help you. I only keep enough money to live on for a few months in here. The rest of my money is in the free world where it is making money while I sleep. Remember, money is only a tool that you use to make your life better.

How Much Money is Enough?

THE MILLIONAIRE PRISONER: PART 3

As a prisoner, your number is much different than someone in the free world. For those of you who have read my first book, *The Millionaire Prisoner*, you know my number was $240,000 or $6,000 a year ($500 a month) for 40 years. You can live like a King in prison on $500 a month. At least in my system we can. Should I win my appeal and get out my number will change. Of course, I will never stop helping my friends or family and growing their money. Some of you may only need $200 or $300 a month? Some of you may want (or need more) to have a bigger pie? That's OK. Whatever your number is you need to find it and write it down. Here's how you find it accurately.

One of the best money books that you can read is *Money: Master the Game* by Tony Robbins. In it, Tony asks a lot of questions and shows you how the successful billionaires did it so you can do it also. So, you can live your dreams. Here's what he said about dreams: "what makes most people just dreamers versus those who live the dream is that dreamers have never figured out the price of their dreams. They make the number so big they never begin the journey." In the book he teaches you how to put a number on your dreams. When you get out you can use the app he created to help you do the calculation. It can be found at www.tonyrobbins.com/masterthegame. Until then, let me show you how to do it by hand.

Tony Robbins lists five financial dreams that you should choose 3 from:

1. Financial Security
2. Financial Vitality
3. Financial Independence
4. Financial Freedom

5. Absolute Financial Freedom

For a prisoner they will be different than someone in the free world who has monthly bills and kids to take care of. So, I'm going to modify them and use two areas prisoner should strive for: *Financial Security* and *Financial Freedom*. Let's look at these two.

To find your financial security number you need to come up with your basic monthly expenses. Get out a pen and paper and your commissary receipts. Do the math and the formula below:

1. Commissary (food, hygiene, envelopes): $____ per month.
2. Phone bill (if you pay it?): $____ per month.
3. Email/video visits bill: $____ per month.
4. Magazine/Newspapers: $____ per month.
5. Tablet/Music/Media: $____ per month.
6. Medical Copays: $____ per month.
7. Court costs: $____ per month
Total $_____ per month.

Total basic monthly expenses: x12 = _____ per year.

Trust me, the number is less than you think. Remember my $500 a month number? I don't need that to have security. My financial security number is closer to $300 a month, or $3,600 a year. That's if I max out my $100 commissary limit each shop. Right now, we are on quarantine due to COVID-19. So, we are only getting one shot per month. That cut my monthly expenses by $100 a month, or $1,200 for the year. Each prison is different. IDOC did away with medical co-pays and cut

THE MILLIONAIRE PRISONER: PART 3

phone costs to 1¢ a minute in the last couple of years. This has helped me and my family out. I can now buy phone minutes at my commissary. Since it is only 1¢ a minute I can put $20 on my phone account and get 100 20-minute phone calls. All my people got to do is accept the call. Even if I used the phone every day that $20 would still last me about three months. Or about $6 or $7 a month. Do the math above and come up with your own numbers. I bet you could be secure if you had $300 a month, or $3,600 a year, while you were in prison?

Now let's move to financial freedom. For a Millionaire Prisoner this means that you have all of your monthly expenses taken care of each month, you have some other money in a growth investment account, and you have a few luxuries. You have all of this and you don't have to work to pay for them. You don't have to be an actual in the bank millionaire to live like a millionaire prisoner! Let me show you how my number is less than the $240,000 I wrote about in *The Millionaire Prisoner*.

At a rate of a conservative 5% a year, you time your monthly number by 20 to get your nest egg. So, for me to continue to live how I have been the last few years I would need: $3,600 ($300 a month) x 20 = $72,000

That's a lot less than the $240,000 I thought I needed. Even if I wanted my original $500 a month ($6,000 a year) I would still only need $120,000. Half of what I thought I needed. So do the math. Add up your monthly expenses and add some luxuries you want. 10 x 8 by 20 and you have your financial freedom number. Got it? Now let's look at how you get that number.

> *"A man who wishes to be rich in a day will be hanged in a year."*
> – Leonardo Da Vinci

Millionaire Prisoner Money Math

To make money, you need to go where the money is. And since I advocate that you can become a Millionaire Prisoner, I want to show you the math behind it. Simply, to make $1,000,000 you must sell:

1 million products at $1 each.
500,000 products at $2 each.
200,000 products at $5 each.
100,000 products at $10 each.
50,000 products at $20 each.
20,000 products at $50 each.
10,000 products at $100 each.
5,000 products at $200 each.
2,000 products at $500 each.
1,000 products at $1,000 each.
500 products at $2,000 each.
200 products at $5,000 each.
100 products at $10,000 each.
10 products at $100,000 each.
1 product at $1million.

As you can see from above, small numbers don't make millions. Look at the numbers above. Which one would be the easiest? It all depends on your product (or service), and who your customers are. Do they have money to spend on your product/service? Do they have the need that your product/service solves? You should ask yourself these questions before you start trying to sell to them.

In 1921, Bruce Burton asked Henry Ford what he'd do if he went broke? The auto tycoon replied: "I'd find something that lots of people have to have and I'd figure out some way to make it better and sell it cheaper than it had ever been made and sold before it. I'd have another fortune before I died."

To hit large numbers of people you need to fish in a pool with a large number of potential customers. Don't forget the hidden potential profit that could come from overseas sales. Yo Gotti made a whole lot more money when his song "Down in the DM" took off overseas in Europe. A 2015 *Publishers Weekly* article illustrated the power in the Chinese market and how two American books have had huge success over there. *The Kite Runner* by Khaled Hosseini has sold over 3.5 million, and *Steve Jobs* by Walter Isaacson has had continued success since it's 2011 release. So, think worldwide, or at least nationally. Ask yourself, can you solve a universal problem?

> *"Go to the ocean with a teaspoon or bucket; the ocean doesn't care."*
>
> – Foster Hubbard

In *The Ultimate Side Hustle Book*, Elana Varon lists 450 moneymaking ideas. Here are the ones prisoners could do from their cell:

Lesson Plan Creator	Essayist
Book editor	Caricature Artist
Survey Taker	Freelance Journalist
Business Plan Writer	Cartoonist
Usability Tester	Ghostwriter
Copy Editor	Fiber Artist
Writing Coach	Grant writer
eBook writer	Fine Artist
Calligrapher	Greeting Card writer

Illustrator
Nonfiction Author
Portrait Artist
Novelist
Tattoo Artist
Poet
Affiliate Marketer
Press Release writer
Personal Investing
Proposal writer

Social Media Marketer
Slogan writer
Web Domain Flipper
Textbook Author
Copywriter
White Paper writer
Paralegal
Songwriter
Blogger

Some of these you may need an assistant in the free world to help you out with. But don't let that stop you. I will also give you additional prisoner examples and ideas throughout the rest of this book. Just remember that having a great idea is not enough. You must implement the idea.

> *"Having the world's best idea will do you no good unless you act on it. People who want milk shouldn't sit on a stool in the middle of the field in hopes that a cow will back up to them."*
> – Curtis Grant

There's so much information out there on how to make money. On the GTL Tablet by itself there's enough stuff about making money to keep you busy for years. So, to help you let me suggest a few audiobooks that you listen to.

Think and Grow Rich by Napoleon Hill
Wink and Grow Rich
How to Turn Your Million Dollar Idea Into A Reality by Pete Williams

THE MILLIONAIRE PRISONER: PART 3

Anything by Earl Nightingale

There's so much more. Just go back to chapter 3 and search for some of those that are listed for the tablet. If you don't have a tablet then I recommend two books:

- *Money: Master the Game* by Tony Robbins
- *The Millionaire Fast Lane* by MJ DeMarco

Of course, if you have not read my first book, *The Millionaire Prisoner*, then you'll want to get it also. It has lots of prisoner examples in every chapter.

Whatever you do, don't let a lack of money stop you from going after your dreams. I had nothing when I started. Now I'm on my way to never having to work again if I don't want to. What's the price of your dreams? Do the math first. Then come up with the idea. Then implement it. Then invest your profits. That's the formula. I'll see you at the top.

> *"Information is the key to success. Whether you are giving it or receiving it...Whether you are selling it or buying it, the right information can make you a millionaire."*
> – Jeff Bezos, Amazon.com founder

CHAPTER SIX

How To Attract Good Luck
"Luck is the residue of design."
— Wayne Allyn Root

This chapter is short, but powerful. Pay attention.

Maybe it's the Irish side of my bloodline? Or the fact that I've always been good at betting on sports? People (especially my fellow prisoners) always tell me that I'm lucky. The reason it looks like luck is because they don't see the hours of studying practice I put in every week. Is it lucky to put in five or six hours every day to write this book? No, instead it's hard work. That's how I get lucky. Here is how you can prepare so that you get a lucky break also:

- Write out your goals. Then write down your specific plans to reach each goal. Go over your goals and plans every week to check your progress.
- Do something. Lots of it. Practice your craft. Be prolific and produce. Learn from your mistakes. Babe Ruth had more strikeouts than home runs. Michael Jordan missed thousands of shots in his career. But both of them are Hall of Famers and remembered for their successes.
- Relax and don't take things too seriously. Life is a game. Have fun and embrace that reality.

THE MILLIONAIRE PRISONER: PART 3

- Read different magazines, books, and newspapers than what you're used to. Talk to different people. Watch different documentaries and TV shows. Get outside of your comfort zone and look for opportunities.
- Put yourself in the right places to be seen and to meet the right people. That means writing letters, getting on line and networking with other successful people. Talk to other cellpreneurs if you have some around you? Form a mastermind group.
- Keep going in the face of adversity. Persevere. Even if no one has answered your first 5 letters write 5 more. Even if no one has bought your first book, write another one. If no one has bought your first painting, paint 10 more. Failure is only failure if you give up. Your success is just around the corner. Or on the other side of the hill. You'll never get there if you quit.
- Pay attention to your intuition and gut feelings. How many times have you met someone and had a bad feeling? Then later on you realize that they were a liar, con artist or thief? That was your instinct telling you to leave. Learn to heed an listen to your hunches. Most of the time it's your subconscious telling you something important.
- Help others without expecting anything in return. Share. Each one to reach one. Give back. Karma is real. So pay it forward. That way the universe will give you more.

For more about getting luck on your side here are some books you may want to get in study:

- *The Luck Factor* by Dr. Richard Wiseman
- *How To Attract Good Luck* by A.H.Z. Carr

CHAPTER SEVEN

How To Get Free Money

*"You don't have to make money back the same way
You lost it."*

– Warren Buffett

The first place to start is with your family and friends. If you've been building your network, you should have some people you can ask? Some of you know that I originally self-published my first book, *The Millionaire Prisoner*. I used $3,000 from a family member to start my publishing company. I actually asked for a loan, but they said I didn't have to pay it back. I haven't looked back since. Here's a few secrets to remember when requesting money from family and friends:

- Ask them to pay for supplies or books that will help you learn and perfect your craft;
- Have them send the money to the supplier or book company (or Amazon.com) and not to you;
- Don't ask them for money they don't have and force them to say no;

Let's look at these. A lot of people won't give prisoners money because they don't know what it will be used for. But if they can put the order in for you, they may say yes? What

THE MILLIONAIRE PRISONER: PART 3

I used to do before I got on was fill out the order form and send it to my family or friends so they could write a check and mail it in. Or just order it online for me. It always worked because they'd rather do that then send me money I might blow on candy and cakes from commissary. Here's what I'd say:

> "I'm sending you this order for several reasons. One, it just takes too long for my prison's trust fund office to process orders. By the time they do it my ADD mind will have moved on. Two, and the main reason, is because I'm tired of being dependent on you for money. It's not your fault I'm in here. So, I want to better myself and learn how to make my own money. Plus, this way I won't blow the money on coffee and cakes from commissary."

Remember to never ask for money they don't have. There's a big difference between money they *won't* give you and money they *can't* give you. A lot of us come from poor families. So, we can't ask for $10,000 to start our own business. But we may ask for $50 to order some books? Know beforehand if they can afford your request.

Another tip is to time your requests. I've been more successful on my birthday, Christmas, and tax check time. The key is to show them their money is being used for the greater good. Don't burn your bridges, build them. After you have asked your family and friends it's time to branch out. There are other sources of money. The two main ones are grants and crowdfunding.

Grants and foundation assistance. It took him six months of filling out applications, writing essays, begging, pleading, and selling, before he landed a scholarship for one class. That was his start, and he walked out of prison with not one, but two degrees, and a 4.0 GPA, and designation on both the Dean's and President's list. Troy is now a professional speaker and author. For more information about Troy and his life, have someone check out his website: www.troyevans.com, or read his book, *From Desperation to Dedication: An Ex-Con's Lessons on Turning Failure into Success.*

> *"There is absolutely no reason why you cannot secure funding while incarcerated. It is only a matter of beating the bushes. The money is there, but the effort has to be there to make it happen... I'm living proof it can happen; you only need to want it bad enough."*
> – *Troy Evans*

Do you want it bad enough? You should, because it's a key to a better life.

Free Money From the Government?

You may have seen the infomercials selling books saying you can get "free money" from the government? In research for this book I had my assistant go to the federal government's official website (https:www.usa.gov) and download what it said about "Government Grants and Loans." Here's what it says:

The federal government does not offer grants or "free money" to individuals to start a business or cover personal expenses, contrary to what you might see online or in the media. Websites or other publications claiming to offer "free money from the government" are often scams. Report them to the Federal Trade Commission.

The government does offer federal benefit programs designed to help individuals and families in need become self-sufficient or lower their expenses.

A grant is one of the ways the government funds ideas and projects to provide public services and stimulate the economy. Grants support critical recovery initiatives, innovative research, and many other programs.
The federal government awards grants to organizations including:

- State and local governments
- Universities
- Research labs
- Law enforcement
- Non-profit organizations
- Businesses

The intent of most grants is to fund projects that will benefit specific parts of the population or the community as a whole. What you might see about grants online or in the media may not be true. The federal government does not offer grants or "free money" to individuals to start a business or cover personal expenses. For personal financial assistance, the government offers federal benefit programs. These programs help individuals and families become financially self-sufficient or lower their expenses.

To search or apply for grants, use the federal government's free, official website, Grants.gov. Commercial sites may charge a fee for grant information or application forms. Grants.gov centralizes information from more than 1,000 government grant programs.

The federal government also provides loans for a specific purpose such as paying for education, helping with housing or business needs, or responding to an emergency or crisis.

Loans are different than grants because recipients are required to repay loans, often with interest.
The federal government offers several types of loans, including:

- Student loans
- Housing loans, including disaster and home improvement loans
- Small business loans

You can search for loans on the federal government's free, official website, Govloans.gov, rather than commercial sites that may charge a fee for information or application forms.

So that's what the federal government says on their website. What does it mean for you? It means unless you are starting a business you probably won't use the federal government's money. That's okay. There are plenty of other sources available to get "free" money from.

Where to Find Free Money?

One easy way is to try www.fastweb.com. Fastweb is a database of more than 180,000 private sector grants and loans and will let you match yourself to the grants that fit your project for free.

THE MILLIONAIRE PRISONER: PART 3

Another great source is the Foundation Center (www.fdncenter.org). After Troy Evans put me up on game about free money, I had my assistant research The Foundation Center. They have a multitude of resources they publish, including the following directories:

- Directory of New and Emerging Foundations
- Foundation Grants to Individuals
- National Directory of Corporate Giving

These directories are expensive. You can access these directories online on the Foundation Center's website for a monthly fee. Check your prison's library first to see if they have any of them? Someone could also look at these directories for free in The Foundation Center's regional offices. They also have 200+ cooperating libraries where you can look at these directories for free. You can find those addresses at www.foundationcenter.org.

You can find local foundations within a specific geographical area through the Council of Foundations (www.cof.org). Or the Regional Association of Grantmakers (www.rag.org). You may also try the Funding Exchange (www.fex.org).

For government money you'll want to search the already mentioned www.Grants.gov or FirstGov.gov. The Catalog of Federal Domestic Assistance (www.cfda.gov) is a database listing information about federal assistance programs. The National Endowment for the Humanities (www.neh.gov) and Institute of Museum and Library Services (www.imla.gov) both support arts and humanities. Lastly, the Community of Science Funded Research Database (www.cos.com) allows you to search grants awarded by five different agencies.

*If you're an artist and you have no one to access the internet for you I list most of the addresses you need to get started in *Prison Picasso 2*. But it's a lot easier to use the web. Here's what funding expert Ellen Liberatori says in *Guide To Getting Arts Grants*:

"Access to public grants has always been very good, in my opinion, and my interaction with government staff has always been very helpful. Nowadays, access couldn't be easier with the Internet and instead of chasing around for public grant opportunities, you can simply put your name on an e-mail list and the grant notice will come directly to you."

That's why it's very important for you to get your email access set up. That way you can make things easier on yourself. Go back and read the "Your Network Is Your Net Worth" chapter if you don't remember. Even after you find possible sources for free money, you still have to ask a certain way. As my big homie tells me, "Come correct or don't come at all."

How To Win Grant Money?

Notice that I said "win" grant money. There will be other people applying for the same grants. It's a competition. Whoever stands out the best with the most compelling application will win. But you have something going for you. That special something is the fact that you're a prisoner. Hardly any other prisoners in the American gulag will try to win grant money so you'll already stand out. So, with the right mindset and the proper grant application/proposal you can find the money to advance your career. Here's what you need to know and what you need to put together.

1. The first thing you have to do is research and apply for only the grants you are eligible for. Some grants have age restrictions, geographical restrictions, specific type of business restrictions, education (alumni) restrictions, gender restrictions, and/or all of the above. Do not waste your time applying for grants that you are not eligible for. Use a website like fastweb.com to find the grants that you are eligible for.

2. After you have found a grant that you're eligible for you have to find out what their application process is. Do they have a form on line that you're supposed to use? If so, you have to use that form and fill it out properly or you will automatically disqualify yourself from the grant process.

3. If the Thunder doesn't have a formal application you need to prepare proposal package that makes you stand out from the crowd. A typical grant proposal will consist of the following:

- Cover Letter
- Title Page
- Abstract/Summation
- Introduction
- Statement of Need
- Objectives
- Procedures
- Budget
- Future Funding
- Appendix

4. Your proposal should be typewritten or done on a computer. If you have no choice but to do yours in your own handwriting then make sure it's done on plain white typing paper and the handwriting is absolutely legible. Prepare it like you were doing an appeal brief to the court.

5. Make sure your proposal is submitted in a timely fashion. Most funders have specific deadlines that you have to meet. Try to get your proposal in early. It's also good to include a SASE or postcard that the funder can return to you saying they received your proposal. Some funders require that be included to pay attention.

6. Remember what I said about asking your family and friends for money: don't ask for money they can't give. This applies to foundations, corporations, and other funders. So, ask for moderate amounts from different sources. Do your research and know how much money they have given in the past.

In the future, The Cell Block will put out a "free money" book all about getting it. If you're an artist/crafter in prison and want to get the addresses of places you can contact to try and get funds, be sure to get my new book *Prison Picasso 2*. If you don't want to go through the process of trying to win a grant, that's fine. I have never got a grant (besides that original gift from my family member). I'm doing fine. The goal is to get where you're making thousands of dollars (if not more) from your ideas so that you don't need a grant. Besides, there's another way to get money that should be a little easier to get than a grant. We'll look at it next.

THE MILLIONAIRE PRISONER: PART 3

The Power of Crowdfunding

You've seen the stories on TV, read about them in magazines, or heard about how some people have used crowdfunding websites to raise money. Author Seth Godin raised $287,342 for one of his book projects on Kickstarter. Brainard Carey, and his wife Delina, used Kickstarter to raise $16,000 in 2011 for their non-visible art concept. Singer Amanda Palmer raised $1 million on crowdfunding. Even projects that benefit prisoners have found success. Chef Bruno Abate used IndieGoGo to raise almost $5,000 to help buy a pizza over for his "Recipe for Change" program at the Cook County Jail. The Human Rights Defense Center (HROC), which publishes *Prison Legal News*, raised almost $15,000 to help fight toxic prisons. Claudia Whitman used IndieGoGo to raise $2,600 to help with a wrongful conviction investigation. In this subsection, we'll look at how a cellpreneur could use crowdfunding to get the money they need.

What is Crowdfunding?

It's a way to raise money for a specific cause or project by asking a large number of people to donate small amounts in a relatively short period of time. Crowdfunding is done online where it's easy for supporters to share a cause or project with their social networks. Organizations, businesses, and individual people (yes, prisoners included) alike can use crowdfunding for any type of project.

There are two main models of crowdfunding:

- Donation-based funding, where donors contribute to a total amount for a cause or project. Normally in the model, the donors are promised a small gift in return for helping out.
- Investment crowdfunding, where businesses seeking capital sell ownership stakes online in the form of equity or debt. In this model, individuals who fund these businesses then become owners or shareholders and have a potential for financial return, unlike in the donation model. This became possible when Title II of the JOBS Act went into effect in 2013. But nonprofits generally cannot utilize equity markets.

Some of the best-known crowdfunding sites are GoFundMe, Kiva, Kickstarter, IndieGoGo, and RocketHub. But there are tons of them. Some estimate there are over a thousand crowdfunding sites? Most of them use the same system:

- Let you set up a page to describe, promote, and post updates about your project, especially with video
- Accept online donations
- Are easily and highly shareable on social networks
- Specify the kinds of projects or campaigns that can be on that site (e.g., creative/artistic; entrepreneurial; personal needs; or charitable)
- Charge a percentage of funds raised plus a fee per transaction

Some sites have an "all-or-nothing" policy. What this means is that if you do not reach your monetary goal, you don't get any of the funds you raised. So, before you sign up to use a crowdfunding site, make sure you read and understand its guidelines, terms, and conditions beforehand.

Also keep in mind that less than half of all crowdfunding campaigns don't reach their goals. Some experts say it's as low as 15-30%. To help you reach your funding goals I will now share with you how a cellpreneur can set up a successful crowd funding campaign.

The Successful Crowdfunding Plan

The first step is to understand that numerous people before you have been successful using these sites for their own projects. A prisoner I know used Kickstarter to raise a few hundred dollars so he could buy art supplies off the commissary. So, the first step is believing it's possible. Here are the others to help make it probable:

Pick the Right Platform.

Different Crowdfunding sites have slight differences in how they fund, how you can promote, the fees they charge, and what types of projects they accept. For instance, on Kickstarter you have to wait till your goal is reached to get your money. But Indiegogo allows you to choose to access the funds as they are raised. Some sites charge 3% of funds raised, but Kickstarter and IndieGoGo have 5% fees, with additional credit card processing fees. The other issue is can you use YouTube and other social networks to promote or do you have to go through the crowdfunding site? All of these areas should be researched beforehand.

Build a Network Ahead of Time.

It would be much easier to meet your funding goals if you have a built-in network of supporters. That's how singer Amanda Palmer raised $1 million. It's how Jerry Mclaughlin and Rebecca Crowell raised $45,000 for their art book project. They used their Facebook community of artists and email list of over 4,000 people. You should use the tips in the <u>Your Networth Is Your Network</u> chapter to build this community.

<u>Make Sure People Know What the Money is For.</u>

This is key. Be specific. For instance, if you need money for art supplies? List them. Don't say, "I need $200 for art supplies?" Say "I need $200 total for the following art supplies." Then list each specific art supply and cost. If it's an art book project, like a comic book or even a how-to book, list each cost along with the total goal. You must do the research ahead of time and know exactly what you need the money for so you can tell your network.

<u>Make Perks Easy and Simple.</u>

It's normal practices for donors to get something in return for backing your project, or cause. You want these perks to be simple with different levels. Let's say you were requesting money for art supplies; you could give the following benefits out:

- $10: public thank-you on Facebook
- $25: hand painted greeting card
- $50: small painting
- $100: 18x24 watercolor painting

Post Updates to Donors.

Let people know and see your progress. For one, it's good karma. Two, you never know where a connection could go. Maybe you'll need more funds down the road? If a donor is happy with how you used the money the first time, they may back other projects in the future.

Use Video

Most successful campaigns use a video to allow possible donors to see who and what they are giving money to. Reread the How to Walk On Clouds chapter for more about doing successful videos.

There you have it. Of course, you'll need someone on the outside to help you with this tactic. But don't let someone tell you it's impossible. Prisoners are using crowdfunding sites to get money for their causes and projects. Maybe you can do it also? Do your research first. Then go get the funding to achieve your dreams.

Additional Resources

If you want to do some more research on how to get free money then I encourage you to have someone order these books for you:

- *The Complete Guide to Getting A Grant* by Laurie Blum
- *Raise More Money for Your Nonprofit Organization* by Anne L. New

- *Securing Your Organization's Future: A Complete Guide to Fund-Raising Strategies* by Michael Seltzer
- *Guerrilla Financing* by Bruce Blechman & Jay Conrad Levinson

If you have a GTL Tablet you may want to listen to the following talks:

- How to Get Private Money
- How to Get Investment Money For Your Online Business
- How to Get Government Grant Money

Just remember. There's money out there. Don't let the fact that you don't have any stop you from going after your dreams. I'm living proof that you can change your life while in prison. It all starts by coming up with ideas and writing letters. You may have a great idea, but who knows about it? This chapter can help you get money for your idea.

CHAPTER EIGHT

7 Ways To Make $$ Off Artwork From A Prison Cell
"A prison is indeed one of the best workshops."
– Sidonie-Gabrielle Colette

As I was reading *Kite* magazine (Issue #5), I saw that they broke down Jay-Z's billion-dollar net worth. That caught my eye because I love reading *Forbes* when they break down the net worth of billionaires. According to *Kite*, Jay-Z owns $70 million wort of art, and in 2013 he paid $4.5 million for Basquait's "mecca" painting. He also has a song on his *Magna Carta… Holy Grail* album called "Picasso Baby" in which he raps the opening bars: "I just want a Picasso in my casa / you know / my castle." I love the fact that *Kite* did that. I just wish they would have broken it down even more. I'll show you why you should follow Jay-Z's lead in this chapter and give you 7 ways to turn artwork into cash (even if you're not the one who does the work.)

The key reason that Jay-Z is buying art is because he understands that it's a collectible asset that grows in value. He understands that valuable assets are investments that make you wealthy. Not spending your money on things that decrease in value as soon as you purchase them. Most of the young prisoners around me only want to get OTS ("off the shit") and read *ATM*'s, *Buttman*'s, and other girlie books. They should listen to Jay-Z's song, *Tom Ford*, where he raps: "I don't pop molly, I rock Tom Ford." And they should pay attention to his investment moves. We all need models. If you want to get wealthy you can't go wrong with Jay-Z as a mentor to look up to. Don't get it twisted, I love to look at a fine piece in an ATM also. But you know what turns me on even more? Cashing royalty checks! Pay attention because I'll give you some ways to get some checks of your own.

In *The Millionaire Prisoner* I listed 10 ways a prisoner could make money off artwork. Of those 10, three of them required a prisoner to get out to start, or a lot of outside help to run. Those three were: open an art gallery, become an art dealer / broker, or be a graphic designer. I won't touch on those ways in this chapter. Instead, I'll deal with the other seven ways you can make money right now off artwork. In research for my latest *TMP* series, *Prison Picasso*, I found that not only are there seven ways still available for a prisoner, but that a lot of prisoners are already taking advantage of them to make money. Remember: the artwork can be yours, or it could be someone else's, it doesn't matter. (If it's someone else's artwork make sure you get a signed contract saying you rightfully own it so you can stay safe from a lawsuit.) Here are the seven ways:

1. Comics/Comic Books/Graphic Novels
2. Children's Book Illustration
3. Posters and Reprints
4. Commissioned Pieces
5. Online Sales
6. Greeting Cards, Calendars and T-shirts
7. Contests

Let me briefly break each one of these down further. If you want a more in-depth look at each one of these seven ways,

THE MILLIONAIRE PRISONER: PART 3

with the complete mailing addresses of companies that can help you, be sure to grab a copy of my newest series, *Prison Picasso 1 & 2*.

Comics/Comic Books/Graphic Novels

I've combined these on the list for simplification purposes. They are really different subniches in one of many art niches. When you think of comics you should think of the ones you see in newspapers and some magazines. My grandpa used to call them "the funny pages." Most of the comics in these newspapers were placed there by syndicates. In the art world, a syndicate is an agent who sells comic strips, panels, and editorial cartoons to newspapers and magazines. So, if you want to see your comic strip in a newspaper you first should pitch your idea to a syndicate. It will be hard for an emerging artist to crack the comic strip code and get it into a major newspaper. To do so you'll have to bump an already existing comic strip. It can be done though.

Another avenue for a cartoonist is to put their comic strip online. You might not make the big money at first, but you could certainly use it for promotional purposes. A top comic strip like <u>Garfield</u>® or <u>Blondie</u>®, can be seen in over 2,500 daily newspapers. Most newspapers pay $10-$15 a week for a daily comic feature. Doesn't sound like much until you do the math. Times that number by the number of newspapers you can get in. At $10 a week in 50 newspapers equals $500 a week. 200 newspapers equal $2,000 a week. And 2,500 newspapers equal $25,000 a week, or $1.2 million a year! Most syndicates split the profits 50/50 with the cartoonist. Of course, you don't even have to go through a syndicate. You can always self-syndicate you own comic strip. That way you would get all the profits. But you'll have to do all the work. It will be a lot harder that way. One way would be to start with the alternative newspapers or weeklies. Then once you break into the market you could go back and pitch your comic strip to the major syndicates.

To submit your comic strip to a syndicate you should have at least 24 of your best samples ready. They should be photocopies of your work, not the originals. These should be on 8 ½ x 11 paper, six daily strips per page. That's a month worth of samples in the comic strip world. You have to submit this number of strips to prove that you can do consistent work, carry the idea and story with it. You should also submit a character sheet with the names and descriptions of your major characters. Lastly, you should have a cover letter explaining your idea. If this is something you want to pursue, here are some books you should consider reading:

- *How to Draw and Sell Comics, 3rd Edition* by Alan McKenzie
- *Comics and Sequential Art: Principles and Practices From the Legendary Cartoonist* by Will Eisner
- *Your Career in Comics* by Lee Nordling
- *Successful Syndication: A Guide for Writers and Cartoonists*

For more resources, books, links, and other sources, you can have someone check out Stu's Comic Strip Connection at: http://www.stus.com/index2.htm

For all the major syndication services you can search www.reuben.org/syndicate.asp

THE MILLIONAIRE PRISONER: PART 3

When I first started doing time, I was a lot younger and didn't know how much to capitalize on great ideas when I heard them. Some 20 years ago in the Joliet maximum-security prison in Illinois another prisoner approached me with an idea for us both to make some money. He saw that I was always reading and writing, and he was a great artist, so he wanted to combine our talents. He was also really into playing football and I was really into watching it and gambling on it. His idea was to do a graphic novel series about football-playing prisoners who were really zombies and vampires. I was too stupid to do anything with his idea.

Years later as I watched AMC's hit TV show, *The Walking Dead*, I cringed. *The Walking Dead* started out as a graphic novel series and was part of a huge zombie craze that hit the entertainment industry. But I totally missed it because I fumbled the ball, he tried to give me. He was a great artist and his preliminary illustrations were awesome. Hey Sleepy, if you're reading this, hit me up, maybe we can still collaborate? But what if you didn't drop the ball like I did and you got a comic book or graphic novel you want to sell? What do you do? Here's what.

1. If you're an avid comic book/graphic novel reader, then you can always look at your own comics to see if their contact information is listed. Write it down and when you're ready, send a SASE requesting their submission guidelines. Or have someone go online and get them. Then put your best work together and send it in.

2. Some prisoners have asked me about the big boys in the comic book world? Like DC Comics®. Most of them don't

take unsolicited submission. To break into DC Comics, you have to drop off photocopied samples of your work at their booth during a comic convention. If DC Comics' representatives like what they see they'll contact you for a discussion on your interests and portfolio. Hey, if you got someone out there who can go to Comic Con, shoot your shot. It only takes one yes to change your life.

If you're interested in doing comic books or graphic novels you could read the following books:

- *The Insider's Guide To Creating Comics and Graphic Novels* by Andy Schmidt
- *Comic Book 101: The History, Methods and Madness* by Chris Ryall and Scott Tipton
- *Making Comics: Storytelling Secrets of Comics, Manga and Graphic Novels* by Marques Vickers

You can also have someone check out these online websites:
    Gocomics.com
    www.comicsreporter.com
    www.the-nose.com

Children's Book Illustration

One of the areas in book publishing that always needs artists and illustrators is children's books. But you need a specific drawing skillset for these types of books. Some prisoners are already creating their own children's books. You could be next? If you're interested in the avenue, then you may want to join the Society of Children's Book Writer's and Illustrators (www.scbwi.org). A great online community to network with can be found at www.childrensillustrators.com. Even though I'll list some of the additional ways to make money with art, if you get your foot in this door you could be set.

How set? It varies and depends on the publisher and the project. Pelican Publishing Company (www.pelicanpub.com) pays $50-$250 per project. Dutton Children's Book which is owned by Penguin Random House pays $1,800-$2,500 per project. Some of the other larger publishers, like Harper Collins Children's Books, won't even work with you unless you got an agent who submits your materials to them. But there are a lot of other publishers who could submit your art to. For an exhaustive list, you should get the latest copy of the book, *Children's Writer's & Illustrator's Market*. (It would be motivational just to get it so you can read all the entries with $ dollar amount for projects. You'll be inspired.)

Posters and Reprints

Some artists produce a piece once, then get paid thousands of times by selling reprints. These are just copies of the original work. You could buy the original paintings form serial killers or other famous prisoners at your facility and offer the reprints for sale online. Or put them into a book and sell copies of the book. Art books filled with reprints go for higher retail prices than regular books. Dr. Nicole Fleetwood of Rutger's University put together a book about prison artists called, *Marking Time: Art in the Age of Mass Incarceration*. It retails for $39.95 and I bought it from Edward R. Hamilton Bookseller Co. for $29.95. I saw other art books in the same catalog selling for $60+! In Buds Art Books catalogs there are art reprint and poster books selling for

$150! There's big money in art books. This could be something you do?

Just be careful if you're not the original creator of the artwork. You could be violating copyright laws if you don't get permission to reuse and resell someone else's artwork. You don't want to get sued for copyright infringement and have to forfeit all of your profits and/or pay damages. It's way simpler just to get permission in writing signed by the other party. (At the end of this chapter I'll give you a simple form you can use for this.)

One of my neighbors did large portraits of Obama when he was in office. He sold them online for $400 each. He put the word "Change" on the bottom of one and it sold as well. These were big 18x24 color paintings. He sold them all for $400. Then someone else approached him to do another one. That's when he told me he wished he had some connections in the art world with an art publisher to make prints of his painting. That way he wouldn't have to keep doing the same painting over and over again. He wouldn't make $400 off a print, but he could sell more prints and make up the difference while he worked on another painting. Of course, I didn't know what an art publisher was, or did, back then. Now I do.

An art publisher is a person or a company that works with you to publish a piece of your art into a print or poster. There are also art distributors, and they are not to be confused with art publishers. An art distributor helps you market a pre-existing print (or poster). Some companies will do both for you. I wish I knew back then what I know now. I could have helped my neighbor and made a little money also. Let's look at some numbers.

THE MILLIONAIRE PRISONER: PART 3

A print is different than a poster. It's a limited-edition print of a piece and is numbered from 1 to 250. Or more. If there are only 250 prints in existence, that would make them collector's editions and highly prized. The prints are made in several different ways. They can be original prints (or by hand), offset reproductions (or posters), giclee prints, and or canvas transfers. A giclee is an inkjet fine art printer. Some publishers print your artwork onto a canvas so it looks like a real painting. Most publishers pay royalties for the prints that are sold. Typically, the royalties are 5 to 20 percent for hand-pulled prints, and 2 ½ to 5 percent for posters. Signed, limited-edition prints average about $175-$200, while canvas transfers sell for $400-$500. Using those numbers, my neighbor would have made $10 off each Obama limited-edition print that sold for $200. That's at the low end of the 5% royalty rate. At the high-end he would have made $40. If his art publisher would have made 250 limited-edition canvas transfers at $400, he would have made $20 off each one at 5% for a total of $5,000. At 20% he would've made $20,000. These numbers make me want to quit writing books and start an art business!

If, and when, you find a company that's willing to work with you make sure you get a contract. Do not sign anything unless you understand it. Because it's your art you have a right to approve a lot of stuff. For instance, you *should* have the final say-so on the size, printing method, paper, number of images to be produced, and your royalty. Some companies don't pay royalties, but instead they pay a flat fee. That's a decision you'll have to make on your own. You should always try to keep complete control of your original artwork. Sell only publication rights. You can also try to put a time limit on how long you'll sell the rights for. That way, you can reuse it at a later date for some other licensing income stream. Posters and reprints can be a lucrative income stream for you if you want. Here's another one.

Commissioned Pieces

If someone pays you money to do a portrait, that's a commissioned work. If someone pays you money for a drawing, that's the same thing. In *The Ultimate Side Hustle Book*, Elana Varon lists 450 money-making ideas. There are eight that I believe a prisoner could do with artwork:

- Calligrapher
- Caricature Artist
- Cartoonist
- Fiber Artist
- Fine Artist
- Illustrator
- Portrait Artist
- Tattoo Artist

She said that "hobbyist calligraphers" charge an average of $150 the design menu for a wedding. Custom documents may sell for as little as $15 for a quote on a poster to more than $1,000 for artwork. There's big money in art. Especially portraits.

A lot of prisoners make a living by doing portraits. Some of them charge $15.00 to $20 a face? I think they should think bigger or outside the cell. One prison Picasso who thinks outside the cell is Salvador Longoria. He advertised in a pen pal publication and offered to do portraits and drawings in any situation. Not only could he build a network of customers that way, but also build his portfolio at the same time. As you get better you could start doing celebrity portraits. In the beginning of 2020, if you could have painted stuff to honor former NBA star Kobe Bryant and his daughter

THE MILLIONAIRE PRISONER: PART 3

Gigi, you could have made a lot of money. People still might buy them? They still buy paintings and drawings of other stars like Elvis Presley, Marilyn Monroe, Michael Jackson, and other dead celebrities. The key is to think about what the public wants. Or just follow the current fad or latest craze.

Andy Warhol started doing portraits for $25,000 each. By the 1980s he was charging $40,000 for portraits he could do in one day! One of my cellmates was making $500 a month off portraits and tattoos. He taught himself how to do portraits and did them in ink so he could charge more. In *Marking Time: Art In the Age of Mass Incarceration*, Rutgers University professor Nicole Fleetwood tells the story of federal prisoner George Anthony Morton. He spent nine years inside and became a master portrait artist. Once he got out, he was accepted into the Florence Academy of Art-United States. Then he became the first American-born student to be accepted into the Florence, Italy campus. All of that happened because of his portrait skills honed while inside a prison. Maybe portraits are your way to some big money? Or to freedom? But you don't have to do portraits. You can draw.

Did you know that there is a magazine that pays up to $4,000 for an illustration? There is. A lot of magazines pay money for artwork they can put in their pages. Do you have any magazines in your cell right now? If you do, pick it up, and turn it to the page where the masthead is. This is normally found in the first few pages and lists the founder, publisher, editors and normally the advertising Department. What you're looking for is the "Art Director" or "Art Consultant." You want that person's name. If you find it, you write it down. That's who you contact when you want to submit artwork for possible inclusion in their magazine.

Before you submit you need to know the lingo of these types of illustrations:

- An "editorial illustration" is a drawing or piece of art that illustrates a story in a magazine or newspaper.
- A "caricature" is an illustration that distorts or over amplifies the features of a person or animal.
- A "spot" is an illustration that is half page or smaller.

The easiest one to break into is spots. They are used to move the readers eyes down the page, or as filler. But if you can do these small drawings well, in your own style, you can make good money. In my book, *Prison Picasso 2*, I list a bunch of magazines that pay good money for art. How good? *AARP the magazine* pays $700 to $3,500. *Brides* magazine pays $250 for spots. *Cave Wall* pays $3,000-$4,000! *Forbes* pays $450-$700. *National Engineer* pays $200 for b/w cartoons. There are many others listed in *Prison Picasso 2*. I hope this inspires you. You don't have to be a painter to become a *Millionaire Prisoner*!

Online Sales

If you really want to take your art career to the next level then you need to start selling online. The Internet offers an avenue to get your art in front of millions of buyers. You need your own website. But you don't have to start there. You could start with Facebook, Amazon, eBay, Etsy and deviantart.com. I first thought about doing a chapter like this years ago when I read about another prisoner using deviantart.com. At the time that site was getting 35 million visitors a month! There are thousands of paintings being sold on Amazon every day. Ebay.com is a major seller of art. Etsy.com is huge for crafters. Are you on any of those websites? You should be if you're an artist or crafter.

I could write a whole book about how to sell artwork online. But I won't because Cory Huff already has in *How to Sell Your Art Online*. He's the founder of TheAbundantArtist.com and here's what he says about it: "The reality is that artists must have a website. It's absolutely necessary. If you want a gallery to represent you, they need to see that you have a body of work. If you want to sell to collectors at large, they need a way of viewing your work, and paying you." He really stresses that you can't rely on art mall websites: "You are an artist, not a commodity. If you were on one of these online art malls, you are one artist among thousands. Browsers will click right by all of your stuff because something flashier is right next to you." Great advice, and a great book. Get it and study it.

Another great book is *The Everything Guide to Selling Arts and Crafts Online* by Kim Solga. For more, check out her website at www.sellingartsandcraftsonline.com.

You could start small with your own Facebook page and work your way up to your own website. Even if it's just a one-page website that points to your art on Amazon.com. That would let you tap into the power of Amazon sales' machine and get your art online. There are other sites to sell art on. Yessy.com sells fine art if you can also sell art on ArtFire.com. Just don't let the fact that you're in prison stop you. There's big money in art. Remember Jay-Z? Most art collectors are sophisticated, smart, and wealthy. Wouldn't you like to have them as your patrons? Online could be the place you start?

Even if you don't have someone to help you build your online platforms at this time there are companies that can help. I know of two that help prisoners sell their artwork online. Caged Kingdom takes 5%, which is what most art gallery's take. I can't vouch for their art selling services, but I have used them for pen pal stuff successfully. And they always respond fast when I send them a SASE. Another place is PrisonArtWear.com. They are a full-service prison art seller and allow you to set up your own portfolio online. I can't vouch for their services, but they look legit. Send a SASE to the below addresses to get their art selling applications:

PrisonArtWear.com
304 S. Jones Blvd., Suite 1683
Las Vegas, NV 89107
(702) 570-9219

Caged Kingdom
4023 Banbury Way
Antioch, CA 94531
cagedkingdom@gmail.com
www.cagedkingdom.net

Greeting Cards, Calendars & T-shirts

So, a story is in order. In 2017 I was debating the easiest and best ways to make legal money from prison with my celly. He kept saying "greeting cards" and I kept laughing at him. Picture a goofy, slow-ass white dude who doesn't get any money and whose cards looked like a 3rd grader did them. Then he said he would bet me that you could make money off greeting cards and he could prove it. The loser would have to make burritos for the other person. I made the bet because I couldn't lose. If he produced, he'd win some burritos, and I'd make some burritos. But I win also because it would be something I could use in future books. If he didn't produce then I got some free burritos.

THE MILLIONAIRE PRISONER: PART 3

After we made the bet, he moved his TV off the property box and went digging around in it. After a few minutes he came up with the Hallmark® letter. When I read it, I knew I was making burritos that night. I also knew that my next book series would be *Prison Picasso*. What the Hallmark® letter said was that they would consider any poetry and greeting card designs for their company. And they would be willing to pay up to $400 for it if they felt it fit their stated guidelines. After I made burritos that night, I went on a research quest to find out more. If this lame could get Hallmark® to write him back, then a great artist should be able to get paid from greeting cards.

From that day forward I started paying attention to greeting cards and the Hallmark letter never left my mind. I saw that some enterprising prisoners are now designing greeting cards and using digital printing technology to reproduce their cards in bulk. That's a great residual income idea. If I was an artist full-time, I would seriously consider creating some catchy icon, logo, slogan, or design, that I could put on everything. I'd put it on T shirts, cell phone cases, books, calendars, mugs, etc. Then as customers ordered the item the product would be created and shipped using the Print-On-Demand (POD) model. CafePress.com and Zazzle.com are the two main POD services for artists. Fine Art America (www.fineartamerica.com) and ImageKind (www.imagekind.com) are POD companies for art prints. InvitationBox.com is for cards. Or put together a book of your original drawings, paintings, and sell it via POD technology using Amazon or Blurb.com. But back to cards.

Instead of selling greeting cards in your cell house for $3 a card, you could license your art to a greeting card company and get paid off of it forever. Some of these licensing companies will also put it on more products, like T shirts and coffee mugs. Some even look for fine art that they put-on limited-edition collectables. The sky's the limit. Here are some tips when submitting your artwork to these companies:

- Do not send your original artwork. Try to get color photo copies made if possible. Some of these companies accept digital JPEGS by email.
- Art should be upbeat and suitable for use in the major Holidays like Christmas, Easter, and Valentine's Day. FYI: Christmas cards account for 60% of the sales in the $7.5 billion greeting card market.
- Make sure your submitted samples are each labeled with your full contact information, including your website and email address if you have them.
- Send four different samples tailored just to that company's market. Include a cover letter and SASE with your samples.

There are other factors that you should consider. Women buy 80% of all greeting cards so your art should be slanted to what women like. There are a lot of greeting card categories and over 3,000 greeting card companies. Pay attention to all of the cards you get in the mail and the ones your fellow prisoners get. Keep a notebook with ideas you see on the cards. Write down the names of the companies listed on the cards. If you really want to take advantage of this market you should consider subscribing to the official magazine of the Greeting Card Association. It's called Greetings, etc. (http://www.greetingsmagazing.com).

THE MILLIONAIRE PRISONER: PART 3

If you want to pursue getting your artwork put on coffee mugs, T shirts, and other merchandise, you should read:

Licensing Art and Design by Caryn Leland. For a complete listing of the companies that license designs and the types of goods licensed you should see if your library has a copy of the directory by the Licensing Industry Merchandisers' Association. If not, it costs $250 from them. (212) 244-1944 or www.licensing.org.

Contests

In *The Millionaire Prisoner 2* I tell the story of a Latino prisoner named "Cocaine" that I met in 2013. He entered a *Lowrider Arte* magazine contest and won best picture with a prize of $400. For a lot of you emerging artists that $400 would go a long way to helping you. Art contests are a great way to build up your resumé also. When entering art contests, you should keep in mind two things: the entry fee, and the rights to the entrant's work. Here's why. A lot of contests charge fees and that's how they make their money. They get all these artists who hope to win paying them fees, but even if they win an award, it hardly means anything. The second problem is that once you pay the entry fee and submit your artwork, the contest owns all the rights to your submission no matter if you win or not. That's why you should always check the contest rules before you submit your work. Here's what Jackie Battenfield says about contests in *The Artist's Guide*:

- Look for shows that don't charge entry fees to enter. You may need to pay shipping if selected, but the jury process should be free.

• Select shows with a specific theme that applies to your work.

• Consider shows open only to regional artists; These can be a good way to expand your connections to your community.

• Most of all, apply only to those juried exhibitions sponsored by an organization you value and trust.

Pretty good rules to follow. But it's your career and your art. You can do whatever you want. Just remember that you're trying to become a <u>Millionaire Prisoner</u>. The object is to go from doing arts and crafts for commissary to making thousands of dollars in free-world money. So never assign rights dear work without first getting paid or having a written agreement saying you still own the rights to the work. Or that you will be paid if the work is sold, which should be put into a signed written agreement as well. I list a bunch of contests that you can enter by mail in *Prison Picasso 2*. You can also find them in some art magazines. Speaking of that.

Top 15 Artist Magazines

You'll need a continuing voice of sound advice, ideas, inspiration, and tips. Since prisoners can't really get online, magazines are a great way to keep up-to-date and informed on the subject matter. Any emerging artist who could subscribe to the below magazines would have an excellent education. Here they are:

THE MILLIONAIRE PRISONER: PART 3

1. *Art Business News*
2. *The Artist's Magazine*
3. *Sunshine Artist*
4. *Art News*
5. *Artforum*
6. *AmericanArtist*
7. *Professional Artist*
8. *Southwest Art*
9. *Modern Painters*
10. *Juxtapoz Art & Culture*
11. *Tattoo*
12. *Pastel Journal*
13. *Watercolor*
14. *Watercolor Artist*
15. *Art in America*

There you have it. Seven ways you can make money off art from prison. There are many more ways. Network with other artists. Read art books and the magazines listed above. You no longer have any excuses. If you choose to keep trading your art for commissary, that's your choice. It's my job to give your ideas and resources that can help you. But it's your job to run with it. Who knows? Maybe in the future Jay-Z will be paying millions of dollars for one of your paintings? I hope so. For an in-depth look at using arts and crafts to achieve your financial dreams, be sure to order copies of my latest books in the Millionaire Prisoner™ line-up: *Prison Picasso 1 & 2!*

CHAPTER NINE

Stock Trading Strategie$

"The stock market is a device for transferring money from the impatient to the patient."

– Warren Buffett

Ever since I read that *USA TODAY* article years ago I have been fascinated by how some prisoners use the stock market to create wealth. There was a prisoner who taught himself to pick stocks. He started out with $1,000 birthday gift from his father. He parlayed that into a mansion, a Lamborghini, and a job at Meryl Lynch upon release. He said all he did was read financial magazines and newspapers and watch CNBC. Then he would phone his father and tell him what stocks to buy and sell.

Another former prisoner who used stocks while inside was Michael Santos. He went to prison back in the 1980s under the cocaine kingpin laws. While inside he wrote a few books, including *Profiles From Prison* and *Surviving A 45-Year Prison Sentence*. Santos made over $100,000 while imprisoned buying Internet stocks like yahoo.com and American Online (AOL).

But there's a difference between reading about other prisoners who were doing it and seeing a convict actually doing it. One of my former cellmates subscribed to the *Wall Street Journal*, *Barron's*, and *Investor Business Daily*. He would order company reports and study them then he would call his parents and tell them what stocks to buy and sell. He never missed a commissary and always maxed out his spending limits. He told me he would never have to work a regular job again because of his investments.

Then I met Jay few years ago. He's a college graduate and former analyst for a Southern Illinois financial firm. He had free-world trading experience and got some time in prison. He was still trading while inside and used RobinHood.com to make his trades. Jay helped another prisoner trade stocks and both lived a whole lot better than most. Stocks are a legal way for you to make money while inside. In this chapter I'll give you some tips to point you in the right direction. It will be up to you to follow through and take action.

> *"You don't need to have a lot of cash in the bank before you start your search for the right investment. Practice first. Practice makes perfect."*
> – Robert G. Allen

Practice Paper Trading

Paper trading is where you practice picking stocks on paper without putting up your money. To do this right you have to be absolutely honest with your picks. And don't fudge the numbers or cheat. Then you'll just be hurting yourself. Here's how you can do it.

- Get a composition notebook (or writing tablet) and pretend you're starting with $1,000 to invest. (I picked this

number because it's what a lot of firms require you to have to start investing.)
- Look at CNBC or in *Barron's* or *The Wall Street Journal* and pick your first stock. Write the date and the price of the stock down in your notebook.
- As you read or see other stocks you like, buy them and put them into your notebook. Remember that you're just practicing. You're not actually buying stock yet. What you're trying to see is if you can actually do it. Or if instead you should let someone else do it for you.
- Set a timeframe of a week or month. Then check your stocks. Did they make money? Did they lose money? Sell your losers and invest in some other stocks. Keep track of those and see how you do.

I used this strategy to learn how to bet on sports. Once I started consistently winning, I started betting small sums. Then I progressed to bigger bets. Now I can make money legally by betting on sports. You can do the same by practicing on paper first.

A lot of brokerage firms offer "visual trading accounts" or "demo accounts" where you can practice for free. Tradingview.com has the paper trading option. They'll put free virtual money in your account so you can invest in practice. Then it will show you in real time how your stocks are doing. Try it out online to see what it would be like to do it for real.

Fundamental Research

Before you start picking stocks and investing your money you should learn about the market. This will give you a firm foundation to lean on as you begin making money in the stock world. Here are some books to get you started:

- *Money: Master The Game* by Tony Robbins
- *A Random Walk Down Wall Street* by Burt Malkiel
- *You Can Be A Stock Market Genius* by Joel Greenblatt
- *Contranian Investment Strategies* by David Dremen
- *The Intelligent Investor* by Benjamin Graham
- *The Warren Buffett Way* by Robert Hagstrom
- *One Up on Wall Street* by Peter Lynch & John Rothchild
- *Beating The Street* by Peter Lynch & John Rothchild
- *Common Stocks and Uncommon Profits* by Phillip Fisher
- *Buying Stocks Without a Broker* by Charles Carlson
- You should also subscribe to the following magazines and newspapers:
- *The Wall Street Journal*
- *Forbes*
- *Kiplinger's Personal Finance*
- *Barron's*

In *You Can Be a Stock Market Genius,* Joel Greenbatt says, "In fact, *The Wall Street Journal* is the hands-down winner for the best source of new investment ideas... You certainly can't (and don't want to) read everything so, just as you do with stocks, pick your spots. Remember, it's the quality of your ideas, not the quantity, that will result in the big money."

I agree. Once you get the foundation you should start small and invest only what you can afford to lose. Never more. Playing the stock market is a zero-sum game. For every winner there has to be a loser. Even the best stock pickers get stuff wrong sometimes. So don't bet everything on one stock pick. Here are some more tips to keep in mind:

- Don't chase the herd. The masses are asses. Don't make investment decisions based on what's popular. Buy low, sell high is still the way to make money.

> *"The object of life is not to be on the side of the masses, but to escape finding oneself in the ranks of the insane."*
> – Marcus Aurelius

- From the great investor Sir John Templeton: "never buy a stock because you like it. Buy it because it's a better bargain than any similar stock you can buy anywhere in the rest of the world. See the investment world as an ocean, and buy where you get the most value for your money."
- Don't fall in love with your investment. Knowing when to get out is the other part of "sell high." Take your profits and buy other stocks to make more money.
- Don't try to wait out a bad stock and cost yourself more money. A loser is a loser. I watched my friend Tim as he tried to hold a stock that he had invested over $3,000 in. He thought it would go back up. It never did. His baby momma never forgot that. Hopefully, he never does either.
- Diversify your stock picks. This means to pick stocks in different industries. For instance, Nike®, Coca-Cola®, and Ford® Motor Company are in different industries. This way if one industry is down all your stocks shouldn't be down.

- At the same time, buy what you know and understand. Don't try to keep finding stocks in stuff you know nothing about. In your free time you can learn more. For now, stick to your experiences.
- Don't try to time the market or "day trade." Pick your stocks and watch them grow in value. Stock prices go up and down every day in increments. If you day trade you could abandon ship the day, or week, before your stock jumps to an all-time high.
- Ignore the news, financial talking heads, and your friend's stock advice. Listen to Warren Buffett, Ray Dalio, Jack Bolge, and other billionaire dollar investors.
- Never invest money you need on stocks! The market is not a get-rich-quick scheme. Stocks are not lottery tickets. Most experts will tell you to keep six months' living expenses in an FDIC-secured bank account. Then you can invest the rest of your money in a diversified portfolio.

My advice is for you to take 50% of your money and put it in a well-diversified portfolio that utilizes low-cost index funds that track the market. Vanguard (www.vangaurd.com) and Fidelity (www.fidelity.com) are two of the more popular places to invest in index-funds.

Then take your other 50% and pick stocks. Remember to us the strategies and tips above. Do your research. Pick your spots and go after your dreams.

> *"To have unconventional success, you can't be guided by conventional wisdom."*
> – David Swenson

How To Never Lose Money When Investing

What if I told you there was a way you could invest in the stock market and never lose money? And the person you gave your money to would guarantee your principle? So, if you gave them $10,000 to invest you could never lose it, but if they make money, you get the majority of the profits. Would you, do it? If you trusted the person, you would. Let me show you how it's possible to do just that.

You do it by using insurance annuities. There are many different types of annuities, but the ones I'm writing about are called "deferred annuities." Of these, there are three types:

- Fixed annuity
- Indexed annuity
- Hybrid "indexed" annuity

Please note that I'm not talking about "variable annuities." Pretty simple definition of what I'm going to show you is a "fixed index annuity" (FIA). Here's what happens.

You give the insurance company your money to be placed in a FIA account. That money is guaranteed. You can never lose it no matter what the stock market does. Then the insurance company invests your money. If the market goes up, you keep the majority of that %, while the insurance company gets a small % of it. Then your profits are added into your original investment and locked in. That means you can't lose it no matter what. After a certain amount of time, you click on your annuity payments and you get income for the rest of your life. The longer you wait to click on your income the more money you'll have. If you want a guaranteed way to invest in the stock market without losing any of your money then you should look for a fixed indexed annuity. You can even start with as little as $500! For more, have someone check out www.lifetimeincome.com.

Recommended Listening

For those of you who have a GTL Inspire™ Tablet, you can listen to all kinds of talks about investing and stock trading. Here are a few to get you started:

- Stock Market Success System
- Stock Market Guide
- Stock Market Investing Advice
- Stock Investing Beginners Guide
- The Stock Market Today
- John C. Bogle
- Peter Lynch
- Warren Buffett
- John Templeton

One Final Thought

> *"If you are ready to give up everything else and study the whole history in background of the market and all principle companies whose stocks are on the board as carefully as a medical student studies anatomy – if you can do all that and in addition you have the cold nerves of a gambler, the sixth sense of a clairvoyant and the courage of a lion, you have a ghost of a chance."*
> – Bernard Baruch

Bonus Section

In *TMP* part 1 I asked a question, "Why rob a bank when you can own one?" You can do that by owning bank stocks. Another way is to become the bank yourself. One of my homies put me up on a book called *How To Invest In Debt* by Michael Pellegrino. It's a great book and I encourage all my fellow up and coming Millionaire Prisoners to read it. Until you get that opportunity, let me share one avenue you could use now: peer-to-peer lending. Essentially, what that is talking about is loaning money to the everyday person without involving a bank. Lending Club is the largest online peer-to-peer lending company. It's also a public company traded on the stock market: Lending Club = LC. So is: On-Deck Capital = ONDK. You can make microloans of $25 to a bunch of different people in need and get a return better than a bank offers you. If this interests you be sure to read the following books:

- *A Beginner's Guide to Lending Club* by Adam Davidson
- *Building Wealth Through Peer-to-Peer Lending* by David Shipman
- *Cutting Out the Banks With Peer Lending* by Dale Poyser
- *How To Profit From Peer-to-Peer Lending* by Scott Todd
- *Understanding Peer-to-Peer Lending* by Peter Renton

But there are other ways to make money off debt. Any prisoner who is going home in a few years should read the below books. They will open your mind to a whole new way of looking at how to become wealthy by using the same secrets the bank uses. Which leads me back to the same question, "why Rob a bank when you can own one?"

- *The Investor's Guide to Buying Debt* by Richard L. Shell & John P. Pratt
- *Bailout Riches!* By Bill Bartmann
- *Fast Cash, How I Made A Fortune Buying Notes* by Lorelei Stevens
- *Billion Dollar Blue Print* by Stephen Gardner
- *Tax Lien Investing Secrets* by Joanna Musa

CHAPTER TEN

Sports Handicapping Succe$$

"They play the star-spangled banner everyday."
— Lem Banker

There are two ways to use sports handicapping while in prison. First, you can bet inside prison against your fellow prisoners. Or you can bet online for real money and not commissary. The principles in this chapter apply to both systems. It's up to you to choose which one you use. If you've never bet on sports before I would suggest starting small before you start making $1000 bets. If you have an addictive personality, I advise that you stay away from this avenue. It takes a lot of discipline to make money in sports betting. It's possible. Let me show you how.

The Number One Rule For Succe$$

Hands down, the most important rule in sports handicapping is money management. Here's a story to illustrate this. For years I had beat my prison bookies. In my prison system they pass out parlay tickets. Different gangs run them under different names, like "Goldmine", "Ubet", "RedAlert", and any other catchy name they can think of to use. The rules are simple. You pick a minimum of 3 games (or 4) and put up a dollar to win $6 (pick 4 = $10 - 12). If one

THE MILLIONAIRE PRISONER: PART 3

team loses, you lose. You have to win all your games. Truthfully, parlays are sucker bets. Vegas gets rich off football parlay cards. Prison bookies get rich off them also. I know, because before I started writing books, I used to run a parlay business for years. Because I made money for years in prison, I thought I was ready to bet online. So, I took a $736 royalty check from one of my books and opened up an online account to bet. First week of the college football season. I had a game I loved. I put the whole $736 on that game. I lost. What was my mistake? If you said I didn't manage my money correctly then you're right. Here's the number one rule:

> No one bet should have the power
> To take you out of the game!

That loss taught me a lot. It showed me that betting in prison is different than betting in the free world. My team actually won the game but didn't cover the spread. So, I lost. Vegas' lines and odds are sharp. Prison bookies lines are soft. I realized that I had to become sharp if I wanted to win against Vegas. I had to set up a system that I followed rigorously. That would allow me to win in the long run. It all started with my mindset. To win at sports betting you have to think differently than everyone else.

> *"The masses are asses."*
> –Wayne Allen Root

Seven Keys To Think Like A Winner

Your mindset is the foundation to success in sports betting. A successful one is a profitable one. That's the Millionaire Prisoner mission – to help you make money. If you just want to have fun and bet your friends on a weekend of NFL games this chapter probably isn't for you. If you want to win money then pay attention to these 7 keys. Implement them into your life.

1. <u>You must take responsibility for your results</u>

If you're not winning then you're doing something wrong. Yes, you will lose. All professional betters lose. But if you lose consistently it usually means it's your system that's producing those losses. Don't get down on yourself, just take responsibility and change it. That's what winners do.

2. <u>Be in it for the long haul</u>

Sports betting is a marathon, not a sprint. As legendary handicapper Lem Banker says, "they play the star-spangled every day." You don't have to bet every day. There will be another game. You have the power to pass on a bet. Also, if you're in it for the long haul, one loss won't affect you as much. All that matters is that at the end of the season you show a profit.

3. <u>Believe in yourself!</u>

Yes, you can win at handicapping. But you must believe it. And it all starts inside of you. Think like a winner. Then behave like one. This is called behavioral congruency. Do what the winners do. Read their books. Study them. Model them. Use their systems. Believe in yourself.

4. <u>Proper preparation prevents poor performance</u>

THE MILLIONAIRE PRISONER: PART 3

Yes, this axiom has become cliché. But it's still true. Think about the hours Michael Jordan practiced and honed his skills. He prepared first. Successful handicappers put in hours of study and research. When at my height in gambling I would spend all week researching my plays for the weekend. That was hours every day in study analyzing a bunch of different factors. I won because of all that preparation.

> *"Victorious warriors win first and then go to war, while defeated warriors go to war first and then seek to win."*
> Sun Tzu, The Art of War

5. <u>Be rational in your decision-making</u>

Life is a series of decisions: what to eat, who to date, what work to do, and what to chase after. Your results are the sum of all the decisions you make. It's the same in sports handicapping. Because that is true, you have to be rational. You have to keep an open mind. You have to manage your emotions. In *Sports Betting to Win*, Steve Ward gives "10 Ways to Help You to Make More Rational Decisions."
Here they are:

- Bet for profits and not for excitement.
- Develop a betting strategy with an edge and commit to sticking to it.
- Emphasize decisions over results and attach pain and pleasure to process of betting, not the outcomes (the money).
- Do your research and utilize statistics and mathematics as a part of formulating your betting decisions.
- Don't bet on your own team (your favorite team).

- Stay open minded and objective and be aware of any biases that may be affecting your thinking.
- Treat every betting decision as unique and independent of every other.
- Manage your risk.
- Only bet when you are "emotionally fit" to do so.
- If life outside of betting is stressful and distracting then take a break.

6. <u>Follow your system</u>

This takes discipline. I didn't do it when I made that original $736 bet. My twin brother told me not to bet that much on that first game. Of course, I didn't listen to him and lost. Money management is just one system. You also need to have a system for coming up with your plays. When the factors don't line up you should pass on the bet. The power is in the system. Follow yours.

7. <u>Look to improve everyday</u>

Remember how I said that sports handicapping was a marathon? That means you get the chance to get better and better at it. So go into it with a child-like mind frame – you want to learn everything you can and have fun doing it. If you look at it like that then you'll learn just as much from your wins as your losses. Practice mastery.

Now that you have the proper mind frame to win at sports handicapping you need to know the process of selecting winning plays.

The Winning Fundamentals

THE MILLIONAIRE PRISONER: PART 3

I want you to come up with your own system. There is power in that. And when you find a winning system you use it until it doesn't work anymore. Don't tell anybody else about your winning systems. You don't want them using them. You want the bookie to keep making the same mistakes over and over so you can capitalize on them. Once they find out about them, they will adjust and you'll have to do the same. Here are some fundamentals that you can use to come up with your own systems.

Have The Best Information Available

Because sports betting was legalized across the U.S. a few years ago it's open season. There are sports books at every casino now. This is a gift and a curse. For one, it means you don't have to travel to Vegas or go online to bet. But it also means that there is a whole lot of information out there that you have to sift through. For starters, you should read and study the following books:

- *The Zen of Gambling* by Wayne Allyn Root
- *10 Keys To A Winning Season* by Phil Steele
- *Sharper: A Guide To Modern Sports Betting* by Poker Joe
- *Good Teams Win, Great Teams Cover* by Pat Hagerty
- *Sharp Sports Betting* by Stanford Wong
- *Lem Banker's Book of Sports Betting* by Lem Banker
- *Beating The Odds* by Brandon Lang
- *Bad Bet* by Timothy L. O'Brien
- *Super Bookie* by Art Manteris
- *The Smart Money* by Michael Konik
- *Swimming With The Sharps* by David McIntire

- *The Definitive Guide to Betting on Sports* by Bruce Millington
- *Sports Betting to Win* by Steve Ward

Those will give you a great foundation and open your eyes to a whole new world. If you can, watch FS1's "FoxBetLive" or ESPN's "Daily Line." Every once in a while, they give out quality information. You don't watch those shows to necessarily get pics. You're watching and listening to try and grab information that you can use later on. My mentor once told me, "Don't pay attention to their picks, but instead to the reasons behind the pick. That's where the gold is at."

The best information is online. Two places to start would be on
http://forum.thegamblingforum.com
http://www.sportsbookreview.com/forum

There are others. As time goes on there will be a lot more sites pop up. By using quality information, you can beat your prison bookies easily. Especially at basketball.

Online Sportsbooks

A lot of states are now legalizing sports betting. Because of that there are some opportunities to make money off their competition. For instance, I live in Illinois. Right off the top of my head I can name five online sportsbooks that Illinois people can bet on:
Pointsbet.com
Betonline.AG
Draftkings.com
Fanduel.com

THE MILLIONAIRE PRISONER: PART 3

BetRivers.com

They all offer sign-up bonuses for new customers. Some offer $250 match bonuses. What that means is that on your initial deposit of $250 they will put an additional $250 into your account that you can bet with. Some also offer free bets. Fanduel had a promotion where you could bet $5 and win $125 on your first bet. DraftKings had a promotion where if you deposited $5,000 they would add $1,000 to your account. You may be wondering why they would do this? Because they are trying to get new customers by enticing them with special deals. Just business 101. The other reason is because they know most bettors will lose all the money in their accounts. If you want to compare all the online sportsbook's bonuses you can at www.oddstrader.com.

If you're considering betting online, make sure it is legal in your state first. Also check out your prison's rules. I'd hate to see you go to seg because you're placing bets over the phone. That could be a good grievance to file if that did happen to you though.

Whatever you do, just remember to go slow and don't bet all your money on one bet. Remember how I lost my whole $736 on one game when I first started? A tough lesson I had to learn. Don't make the same mistake. Here's some more tips.

Line Moves

When I read the book *Smart Money* by Michael Konik, I became aware of line moves. There are big betters out there who can move lines on games. Joe Public could walk into a sportsbook and bet $100,000 on a game and the line won't budge. But if a well-known professional gambler does the same thing it could move the line a half point, or more, depending on the circumstances and bettor. Because of this I started following major line moves. You can do this online at VegasScoresandOdds.com or on the DonBest.com website. It will show the "Opening Line" and the "Current Line". For instance, on January 23, 2021 I called home at 2:30 pm and had my girl check out VegasScoresandOdds.com for the NBA lines. Here's what they were:

Team	Opening Line	Current Line
Utah	- 6 ½	- 7
Philadelphia	- 8 ½	- 7
Brooklyn	- 8	- 7 ½
Los Angeles	- 9	- 9
New Orleans	- 7	- 5 ½
Dallas	- 10	- 9 ½
Denver	+ 1 ½	-2 ½

If you would have bet with the line moves you would have went 6- ATS (against the spread). Look at New Orleans. They opened as a -7 favorite. By the time I called they were down to a -5 ½ favorite. That means either there was professional money coming in on Minnesota (New Orleans' opponent) with the points, or there were injuries. Or both. Final score: Minnesota won head-up 120-110. So, anyone who took Minnesota plus the points won their bets. There's a phrase for following the smart money: chasing steam. You can make a lot of money by betting with the line moves.

A word of caution: don't blindly bet with the line moves. Do your own research first. Then check the line moves after. That way you can see if you're betting with the

THE MILLIONAIRE PRISONER: PART 3

smart money? Or see something you're missing. This is one more factor to add to your handicapping arsenal. In prison, you can use this tool to beat your cellhouse bookies. Why? Because they will typically put out their lines and parlay cards as soon as ESPN displays the lines at 11am. If the games don't start till 6pm you have enough time to call home and check line moves. I did it on January 23, 2021. My prison bookie made No -8 at Minnesota in NBA. When I called home and saw it was No -5 ½ I knew I had vale at +8. Research is how you win at this game. Never forget to research major line moves.

Picking Basketball Winners

This is where I used to kill them. One guy used to call home to get the lines. Then he would put out his numbers. By the time it was tip-off I could usually pick off his bad numbers. All I did was keep my own power ratings and do simple math and when his number was 3 or more points off, I'd bet. I made so much money that he would ban me from betting. Then I'd go find a few people to put in bets for me. It was a daily grind. A lot of experts will tell you to pick one sport and master that. If I was advising you, I'd tell you to pick basketball.

Joe Public, i.e., "the masses of asses", love NFL football. That's what they grew up betting on. But the advantage is on the linemaker for NFL. The games are once a week so the bookie has time to adjust. Not in basketball. When you factor in the 300+ college teams, you have a lot of opportunity to make money throughout the season. Vegas knows this and limits the amount you can bet on basketball. NBA may be

$5,000, while college may be $3,000? That's okey. I'll take $5,000 wins all day. Won't you?

The classic book to read is *Basketball: Picking Winners Against the Spread* by A.J. Friedman. It was published in 1978 by Gambler's Book Club Press and is still being sold by them. That's how good it is. All you would need is a basketball schedule, a calculator, some pen and paper, and you could track your own numbers. You come up with your Power Ratings before the season starts and then you adjust them every night after the last game goes final. Or you pay someone else to do it for you. I used to do it on my own because I liked doing it. Maybe you will also?

Money Management 101

The key to it all is to start with a large enough bankroll so you can last the whole season. In my experience, I would set aside $200 – 500 for in-prison betting. If I was to bet full-time in the world, I would start with at least $5,000, but preferably $10,000. I would make sure that I had other income streams as well. That way if I lost all my bankroll, I wouldn't be bankrupt. If you follow the below money management system you should never go broke unless you're just no good at this.

Because it's the easiest math I will pretend you started with a $10,000 bankroll. The most you're allowed to bet on any one bet is 5%. So, $500 is the most. That's not what you should bet every time though. That is just the maximum you're allowed to bet. I would suggest you start at 3% of your bankroll. So, if your bank is $100, your bets will be $3. If your bankroll is $1,000, your bets would be $30. If you just said that's not enough skip ahead to the next chapter. You don't

THE MILLIONAIRE PRISONER: PART 3

have the discipline to do this. Here's how my brother and I used this system to turn $1,500 into $30,000!

Our starting bankroll was $1,500. Our week-one bets are 3% or $45. We make only two bets a day for 14 total bets a week. No more. At the end of week one we raise or lower our bet size. It depended on if our bankroll was up or down. We kept our bet size to 3% of our bankroll, but once we added our winnings to the bankroll our bets automatically go up. For instance, if our bankroll was %1,590 at the end of week one. Our week two bets would be $48 ($1,590 x 3% = $47.70). But if we lost? And our bankroll was only $1,410? Then our week- two bets would be $42 ($1,410 x 3% = $42.30). If you can pick winners more than losers, and have the discipline to stick to your money management system, you can get rich.

Some days you'll lose all your bets. (We only bet two games a day or 14 a week). Whatever you do, do not chase your losses. Don't try to win all your money back on that late-night Hawaii-Nevada football. Get some rest and start anew tomorrow. It's a daily grind. Most people can't do this. They don't have the discipline to do it. If you like sports, like crunching numbers, and have a sufficient bankroll, you can make some good money betting on sports. I'll leave you with a great thought from Poker Joe's book *Shaper: A Modern Guide to Sports Betting:*

"Here is the single best test I know as to whether you're ready to be a pro bettor. Ask yourself, 'Does this idea of betting sports for a living sound *awesome?'*

If you answered 'Yes!'... you aren't ready. If being a pro bettor sounds fun to you, you haven't learned what being a pro bettor *is.* You haven't really thought it out. Think it out. Good luck. Have fun."

CHAPTER ELEVEN
Publishing Profit$

"I would rather surrender two fingers on my left hand then sell all my rights to a manuscript prior to publication. My right hand, with fingers intact, would refuse to sign the contract."

– James A. Michener

This chapter is the easiest for me to write. In the last ten years I have read hundreds of books about writing and publishing. I have started my own publishing business and self-published my own book from a maximum-security prison cell with no access to a phone or tablet. I have also had 4 other books published by other companies. Every 3 months I get royalty checks from Amazon.com and those publishers. I'm not telling you this to brag. I just want you to know that I write this chapter from experience. And since I have done it means you can do it also. In this chapter, I'll give you other examples as well from across America. Many prisoners are using the written word to change their lives for the better. Maybe you can too?

18 Ways To Make Money With Writing

In my first book, *The Millionaire Prisoner*, I listed 18 ways that a prisoner could use the written word to make money. Here they are:

1. Magazine Articles
2. Books
3. eBooks
4. Blogs
5. Booklets
6. Graphic Novels/Comics
7. Syndicated Columns
9. Databases
10. Directories
11. Form Kits
12. Newsletters
13. Special Reports
14. Workbooks
15. Movie/TV Scripts
15. Music Lyrics
16. Copywriting
17. Editing
18. Publishing

I go into-depth about each one in that book, but I've included them here to spark your imagination and get you to think outside the box you live in. Before I get into the actual how-to side of things, let me share with you how other prisoners have used writing to escape the prison and find their destiny.

Prisoner of the War on Drugs

Richard Stratton went to prison during the war on drugs. While inside he started writing books. He wrote the 1990 novel *Smack Goddess*. And he even started *Prison Life* magazine. Some of his other books are *Smuggler's Blues* and *KingPin: Prisoner of the War on Drugs*. Once he got out of prison he became an expert witness in state and federal courts, and has been on HBO documentaries. His latest book is *In The World: From the Big House to Hollywood*.

Another prisoner who used his time to write and go to Hollywood is Eddie Bunker. He used to stay up late into the night at Folsom Prison California to work on his books. He wrote *Straight Time*, which was turned into a movie starring a young, Dustin Hoffman. His autobiography, *Education of a*

Felon, should be required reading for every new prisoner. After he got out of prison he was cast in the movie, *Reservoir Dogs*. You could be the next guy to go from the Big House to Hollywood?

Prison How-To Workout Books

Paul "Coach" Wade entered San Quentin prison at 22 years old in 1979 for drug offenses. He spent 19 of the next 23 years inside some of the toughest prisons in America. Places like Angola and USP-Marion. He used all of his time to work out and got swole using his bodyweight. They started calling him "Entrenador", which is Spanish for "Coach", because all the new prisoners came to him for advice on how to work out properly. For a small fee he started selling his advice. He got the idea for his first book, *Convict Conditioning: How to Bust Free of All Weakness – Using Lost Secrets of Supreme Survival Strength*, when he was in year 6 of an 8-year stretch at Angola Penitentiary ("The Farm") in Louisiana. He took all his notes, ideas, and scribbled training programs wrapped up in a big card file, and turned them into that book. It retails for $39.95 and the eBook is $19.95. His book has evolved into a whole series of books and training videos. There's *Convict Conditioning 2*; *Explosive Calisthenics*; *C-Mass*; and the *Convict Conditioning Training Log*. Those books have been turned into a whole video series as follows:

> *Convict Conditioning*
> Volume 1: *The Prison Pushup Series*
> Volume 2: *The Ultimate Bodyweight Squat Course*
> Volume 3: *Leg Raises Six Pack from Hell*
> Volume 4: *Advanced Bridging: Forging An Iron Spine*

THE MILLIONAIRE PRISONER: PART 3

Volume 5: Maximum Strength: The One-Arm Pullup Series

Each DVD sells for $29.95. That's how you take one book idea and turn it into a whole series of products. For more, check them out at: Dragon Door Publications, INC.
5 East County Rd. B, #3
Little Canada, MN 55117
www.dragondoor.com

> *"In prison, you have to depend on yourself. You need to learn to coach yourself. If being incarcerated in correctional facilities taught me one thing, it taught me the value of living a disciplined, regulated lifestyle."*
> – Paul "Coach" Wade

Nico Walker was a 33-year-old Army Veteran who was sentenced to eight years in federal prison for bank robbery. He wrote his first novel *Cherry* while inside. It won acclaim in *The New York Times* and *New York* magazine.

Michigan lifer Curtis Dawkins is a fiction writer. He started by getting short stories published in a small literary magazine, *Bull*. Those stories were turned into a book, *The Graybar Hotel*, which Scribner paid an advance of $150,000. Unfortunately, the Michigan DOC filed suit to recover the costs of incarceration out of the royalties from his book. (For more about this, see the August 2018 *Prison Legal News*).

Triumph Over Censorship in Prison

In 1987, Paul Wright entered the Washington State prison system to begin serving a 304-month sentence. In 1988 he met

Ed Mead; a prisoner who had been locked down since 1976. They decided to start a newsletter about prison-related legal news. On a $50 budget, they launched their first issue in 1990. They each typed 5 pages in their cell and sent it to a friend on the outside who copied it, and published it. Wright and Mead sent that first 10-page edition of *Prison Legal News* to 75 potential subscribers and they were off and running. Ed Mead was released on parole in 1993 and left *PLN* to do his own thing in California. He's now on the board of directors at *California Prison Focus*. Paul Wright continued to put out *Prison Legal News*.

Did Wright encounter obstacles? Sure, he did. Prison officials tried to stop *PLN* by shipping Wright around to different prisons, banning bulk mail, and even banning the magazine itself. The first three issues were banned in Washington, and the first 18 in Texas. In 1999, Washington prison officials banned correspondence between prisoners which severely limited Wright's ability to coordinate *PLN*. But that didn't stop him from publishing *PLN* because he was determined to get this information out to subscribers.

Paul Wright was released from prison in 2003 after 16 years. He continues to publish *Prison Legal News*, now a 55-page monthly magazine with over 9,000 subscribers in all 50 states and other countries. Did the battles with prison authorities stop once he was released? Hardly so. Prison officials are still trying to keep *PLN* from prisoners, even as *PLN* wins court battle after court battle over the censorship of *PLN*. Wright had a vision for *PLN* and used a lot of persistence to see that dream accomplished. Wright formed the nonprofit organization, the Human Rights Defense Center (HRDC) to help battle unjust censorship and other violations of prisoner rights. He has also launched a sister publication to *PLN*, Criminal Legal News. You can find out more on HRDC's website at: www.humanrightsdefensecenter.org, or *PLN's* at: www.prisonlegalnews.org.

> *"Adversity causes some to break, while others break records."*
> – Harvey Mackay

Diamonds in The Ruff

Ty Evans is an Indiana prisoner serving a 71-year sentence for a 2005 attempted murder and resisting arrest conviction in Marion County. While incarcerated, Evans graduated from Ball State University in December of 2009. In 2012 he published the first edition of the *Indiana PC Guidebook*, a self-help lawbook for Indiana prisoners. Prison officials banned it, not because of anything inside of it, but because he didn't get permission to write it. Of course, he sued them over that bogus denial, and with the help of ACLU attorney Gavin Rose he won the case to get it back inside. See Evans V. Lemmon, USOC Case No. 1:13-cv-00049-LMJ-MJD.

He has continued to write and publish. His articles can be found at *prisonwriters.com*. His other books, under the pen name, Ivan Denison, are *Flipping Your Conviction; Flipping Your Habe; The Essential Supreme Court Cases; Fifty Million Years in Prison*; and *Religious Rights of Prisoners*. Just another Millionaire Prisoner success story who didn't let prison stop him from achieving his dreams.

#BlackLivesMatter

Probably the most famous writer in prison right now is Mumia Abu-Jamal. His story began at the age of 14 when he became a member of the Black Panther Party. He got his degree from Goddard College and a master's from California State University at Dominguez Hills. In 1981 he was elected president of the Philadelphia chapter of the Association of Black Journalists! Then in December of 1981 he was arrested for killing a police officer, who shot him as he ran to help his brother. Bleeding, Abu-Jamal was left lying in a police wagon for almost a half hour. Once he got to the emergency room, he was punched and kicked by police officers. His subsequent trial in 1982 was a gross injustice, where racism in the jury selection process and prosecutorial misconduct ran rampant. The trial judge was overheard saying that he was going to "help fry that nigger." Amnesty International dedicated an entire report to the injustices at this trial. Mumia was sentenced to die. But that's where our story just begins.

From a tiny cell in a Pennsylvania prison, Mumia Abu-Jamal has published many articles, and completed successful books, including *All Things Censored*; *Live From Death Row*; and *Jailhouse Lawyers: Prisoners Defending Prisoners V. the U.S.A.* He has been interviewed by National Public Radio, and phones weekly commentaries to the Prison Radio Project. Because of his own work as a jailhouse lawyer, Mumia was appointed vice-president representing jailhouse lawyers of the National Lawyers Guild. The people of Paris, France named a street after him, and a movie, *In Prison My Whole Life*, tells the story of his case. Considering that he was on death row for over a quarter of a century makes these accomplishments remarkable.

THE MILLIONAIRE PRISONER: PART 3

Abu-Jamal's cell is the size of a small bathroom. He has a typewriter, but the prison commissary jacks the prices of ribbons so high, he must reuse his over and over. This causes the words to be faintly legible on the page for the editor to read. The prison system only allowed him to keep seven books in his cell at one time. He has no access to a computer or the internet. Prison officials punished him for publishing his work and he vowed to never stop writing. His case went before the 3rd Circuit Court of appeals who ruled in his favor. See Abu-Jamal V. Price, 154 F.3d 128 (3d Cir. 1998). Politicians we not done trying to silence Mumia. Just three days after his alma mater Goddard College announced Abu-Jamal as its commencement speaker, Pennsylvania State representatives announced the Pennsylvania Revictimization Relief Act. It was a blatant attempt to silence "one particular killer" as then-Governor Tom Corbett lauded at a bill-signing event near the intersection where Abu-Jamal's crime of conviction occurred. Mumia and other prisoners sued to enjoin the enforcement of the Act. In 2015, Chief Judge of the Middle District, Christopher Conner, in Pennsylvania ruled that the Act impermissibly infringed on free speech, was unconstitutionally vague and overbroad, and a permanent injunction was warranted. See Jamal V. Kane, 105 F.Supp.3d 448(M.D.PA 2015).

The difference between Abu-Jamal and other prisoners is their attitude, daily habits, and determination. While others in prison may have more physical tools, such as books, computers, and email, Abu-Jamal does more with less. He has become a bright and shiny key in this dark prison world. As he says, you can become a "legend or a lizard." Certainly, Mummia Abu-Jamal is a legend, and his story should be an inspiration from behind prison walls, he continues to triumph over bogus censorship practices. He's not the only one.

$10,000 Awarded for Urban Novels

Victor Martin found himself in the North Carolina prison system serving a 23-year prison sentence. So, he started writing urban novels to make some money. He became good at it. So good that a major publisher put out four of his books before 2006. While he was writing from 2002 to 2006, he had no disciplinary infractions and prison officials commended him for "doing something positive." All that changed when Martin was transferred to central prison in Raleigh, North Carolina. Captain Frederick O'Neil, who was then a Lieutenant with the internal affairs office at the prison, searched Martin's cell and confiscated a 310-page handwritten manuscript. Captain O'Neil did not like Martin's writing because it contained "the language of the streets." And he used racist epithets during his interactions with Martin.

During his stay at central prison, Martin was issued 30 disciplinary tickets for writing and publishing. He got a ticket for "conducting a personal business" when his publisher accidentally sent a royalty check to the prison. He spent time in administrative segregation as punishment for his writing and publishing. In 2008, Martin was transferred to the Pasquotank Correctional Institution. Prison officials there did not mess with him for his writing. Because he did not want to go through the mess again, the ACLU on Martin's behalf, filed suit in federal court for violation of his First Amendment rights. In March of 2010, NCDOC agreed to settle the case for $10,000 in damages and a new policy which allows North Carolina prisoners to write for publication as long as they don't receive direct compensation. See Martin V. Keller, USDC (E.D.NC)5:09-CV-0044.

I hope these stories have inspired you. There are many of us around the country who are using the written word to change our lives. Even prisoners across the pond keep writing. Jeffrey Archer was a famous author and a British Lord. At the age of 61, he was sent to prison for lying about being with a prostitute. He did two years in prison where he wrote a three-volume nonfiction trilogy called, *A Prison Diary*. Never give up. Never stop writing. Never stop trying to achieve your dreams. That's the motto of Millionaire Prisoners.

"You're stuck with what you've got, so get on with it."
– Jeffrey Archer

7 Easy Steps To Writing a "How-To" Book

My specialty is how-to self-help nonfiction books for prisoners. Over the years I have developed a system that allows me to write books easier. Using the system, I wrote *Pen Pal Success* in 30 days! Here's my system in 7 easy-to-follow steps:

Step 1 = Pick a topic you know about. The more you know about a topic the easier it will be for you to write about it. Also, you'll already know where to go to find additional information on that topic to make your book better.

Step 2 = Come up with a great title. Great "how-to" book titles have a short catchy title, which is the "grabber". Then they have a longer "descriptive" subtitle. This is done for marketing purposes. *Pen Pal Success* is the short benefit "grabber" title. The long "descriptive" subtitle is *The Ultimate, Proven Guide To Getting & Keeping Pen-Pals*!

Step 3 = <u>Write a full-page ad for your book idea</u>. If you can't do this you can't sell your book and you haven't got a good idea. Who is your how-to book for? That's your target audience. Now write a full-page ad aimed at enticing them to buy your book. Use the ads in the back of this book as examples. What would your headline be? What points would you emphasize in your ad? I do this for all my book ideas before I write one word. Because I know that if I can't do this, I either don't know enough about the subject, or about my target audience.

Step 4 = <u>Draw up your front and back covers</u>. You do this so you can tape these to the folder or notebook that you will write in. In essence, you're building a book. They don't have to be fancy drawings either. When I did this for my first book, *The Millionaire Prisoner*, I just had a photo of a money clip full of hundred-dollar bills I ripped out of a magazine. I taped that to a white piece of typing paper and wrote my title on the top of the page. On the bottom I put my name. Then for my back cover I put a fake barcode with price, my "About the Author" blurb, and a description based off my full-page ad. So, every day I saw these images and was inspired to write in my book.

Step 5 = <u>Do an outline for your book</u>. Some people do a table of contents. I don't do that yet. My outline is more like a "To Do List". If you do TOC first, that's fine. Whatever you do it will be your roadmap to a finished book. Here's the key: do the easiest parts first. That way you build momentum and don't get burned out. I do my Dedication, Warning-Disclaimer, Introduction, About The Author page, and all the other easy stuff first. Remember, you're building a book.

Step 6 = <u>Write a chapter a day</u>. They don't have to be perfectly laid-out chapters. You just want to get in the habit of writing every day. When I did *Pen Pal Success* I was in ad-seg. No TV, no distractions. I did my rough draft of each chapter in the morning and polished them up and perfected them in the afternoon. As I lay there at night, I was plotting out the next day's chapter in my head. While I was asleep my subconscious wrote the chapter. When I woke up, I had to get it all out onto the page.

Step 7 = <u>Put your book away for a week then come back to it and rewrite or edit it</u>. I learned this from Stephen King's book *On Writing*. The key is to work on something totally different, or nothing at all. Go play sports. Goof off. Take a break. Whatever you do, you're not to touch your manuscript. After a week (or longer), you get it out and reread it. Then you tighten up any errors and make your corrections. Trust me, you'll find quite a few, especially if it's the first time you write a manuscript. A good little book to help you at this stage is *Self-Editing On a Penny: A Comprehensive Guide* by Ashlyn Forge.

There you have it. That's the system that I use to write my books. It has allowed me to write 6 books pretty quickly. From 2018 to 2020 I didn't write any books. Once COVID-19 hit I was stuck inside my cell again. there were no sports to bet on so I started writing again. I used this system to do this book, and *Prison Picasso*. We also updated *Pen Pal Success*. You can do anything you want when you put your mind to it and then do it every day!

The Secrets to Creating Income Streams From Your Book!

Years ago, I read a book called *Multiple Streams of Income* by Robert Allen. Ever since then I'm always on the lookout for creating additional streams of income. Here's how you can turn a book into multiple streams of income. First off, this idea is not for most fiction books. Although you should have promotional material at the end of every book, these ideas work best for how-to nonfiction books. I must be honest with you, I stole some of these ideas from *Book The Business* by Adam Witty and Dan S. Kennedy. Combined, they have published over 30 business books. I'm a student of Kennedy's *No B.S.* business book series and highly recommend that you read any of those books that you can get your hands on. If I remember right, I paid about $20 for *Book The Business*. That book gave me an idea that Freebird Publishers and I used to make over $700 before we even sold one copy *of Pen Pal Success*. So, I know these ideas work. All you have to do is put in the work and apply them to your own book.

If you have a copy of the first edition of *Pen Pal Success*, you may notice that some companies have advertisements inside the pages. That was by design. After reading *Book The Business*, I contacted Diane at Freebird Publishers and told her my idea about selling ads in our book to complimentary companies who wanted to reach the prison market. Several companies took us up on our offer and we made over $700 before the book came out. That was a small success, but here's what I should have done:

- Sell ads in the book (which we did);
- Charge other authors a fee to guest write a chapter. (In return they get the publicity and authority for being "Coauthor" of a book);

THE MILLIONAIRE PRISONER: PART 3

- Get paid off each customer who is referred to a company listed in the book if they become a paying customer of that company;
- Start my own pen pal company and use the book to hype that company and build it.

That's what should have been done. One should not reject wisdom because it comes late! So, if you're planning on writing a how-to non-fiction book, think about the side businesses that you could start based on (of from) your book's topic. For instance, any good jailhouse lawyer could put together a post-conviction law book for their state. Ty Evans has done a good job of that with his Indiana PC Guidebook. They could make a deal with a law firm that specializes in those issues where they get paid off referrals from the book. One prisoner wanted to give me $200 to do his post-conviction petition because I was a writer and had a typewriter. Imagine what I could have charged if I had a law book under my belt.

In any prison I go to I'm considered an expert, authority, and celebrity. Why? Because I'm the author of several books aimed at helping prisoners. My name and face are on all of my books. Because of *The Millionaire Prisoner* I'm considered an expert on making money from a prison cell. Because of *Pen Pal Success* I'm considered an authority on how to get and keep pen pals. Because of *Cellpreneur* I'm the go-to guy for advice on starting a business from inside prison. More prisoners come to me for advice because of my books than any other reason. Because of my books I'm a celebrity in my prison. If I was in the free-world I would charge people a fee for my advice. In prison, I'm glad to help out as long as I'm not busy writing or doing research for one of my projects.

Some prisoners come to me with ill intentions or want me to do all of the work for them. They are quickly banished back to a life of oblivion. Even in prison your time is valuable so guard it like your life depends on it.

Michael Santos leveraged the books he wrote while inside federal prison to build a million-dollar real estate empire. He also taught a class at a major Californian University. He offers his services at the end of his books and he's the perfect example of how to use a book (or books) for success. He's now known as "the Prison Professor."

My friend and mentor, Pete Bowerman, does a great job of selling his other services in his books. He calls it "Spinoff City." Bowerman is author of several books, including *The Well Fed Self Publisher*. One of his side businesses that developed from his books is Title Taylor™. In that business he helps authors come up with more profitable titles for their books, along with front and back cover copywriting. He also offers an ezine, coaching, teleseminars, supplementally books, and speaks at conferences. You could also offer affiliate products and services in your book and ebooks in which you get a commission off each sale. Here's a simple way you could do it:

- Think of the services or additional information your readers will need to complete the task your book advises on;
- Contact the companies (or authors) that provides such and ask them if they would give you a fee of each paid customer who you bring to them;
- As soon as you see that enough of your readers are purchasing said products or services you should create your own product or service so that you get the full benefits off that reader/customer.

Think about your how-to book is more than just a book. It's a platform to side businesses and additional streams of income. Done right, that one book could be the way to earn a living without ever having to work a day job again. Learn to think like a Millionaire Prisoner and begin building your income streams before you even sell one copy of your book.

I reached out to Ty Evans to get his thoughts on the whole subject. He wrote me back and here is part of his letter used with his permission. Pay attention to the gems he lays out.

Ivan Denison's 12 Points of Publishing

With regards to publishing in general, I can offer you these insights from my experiences. Call it "Ivan Denison's 12 Points of Publishing":

1) It is vastly important for the self-publishing author to fully control the appearance and content of his work, which will enable the finished product to be given to a person to upload to Kindle (or any other publisher). The Kindle requirements and restrictions are on their website. The computer files should include:
 a. Text in both .doc and .pdf formats
 b. Book cover in .pdf format
 c. Author biography in .doc format
 d. Book description in .doc format

2) Don't fall in love with every word you write. Learn to edit yourself. Revise, revise, revise. Good stuff that hits the cutting room floor can be developed in another project later.

3) Check your verbs. In one phase of my editing process, I take a draft and write in the margin every verb in every line.

Then I seek more vivid verbs, trying to avoid playing verbs like "be, is, was, were, are".

4) Proofread, proofread, proofread. It is immensely annoying to receive your published work and spot a typo in the first 10 minutes.

5) If you don't have something original to say, why even write? Have an insight, and have a point. This goes for both fiction and nonfiction.

6) Don't expect to become an overnight success. Know that 80% of books published by major publishing houses LOSE money; for self-published authors the success rate is even lower. Over 99% sell fewer than 100 copies. It takes practice to become a good writer.

7) Self-help books generate more sales in the long run, and a good self-help book sale actually increase monthly over time.

8) Fiction has a short shelf life. Sales are hot the first month or two, then usually fall to near zero. Only the big-name authors are immune to this, and even then, it is only a matter of degree.

9) If you're marketing the book to family and friends, it is probably to obscure to generate sales to anyone else. And your friends and family probably won't really appreciate being solicited (but they won't tell you that). Personal memoirs are usually dismal failures, so get off the egocentric idea that the world will be enamored with your personal struggles.

10) Advertise only in a magazine that your target audience reads.

11) Write articles for magazines and blogs. Do this cheaply, because it advertises your books. If someone read

your article and likes your writing, they often look up other things you have written.

12) The First Amendment is a sacred right. Use it to expose the truth, to align others, and to be a check against abusive governments – that's what the amendment is for, and why it was listed first among the Bill of Rights.

Writing and Publishing Resources

Before I leave this topic, I would like to give you some additional
books that you may want to check out to help you on your journey.

- *How to Write Urban Books for Money & Fame* by Mike Enemigo & King Guru
- *Jailhouse Publishing for Money, Power, and Fame* by Mike Enemigo
- *Writing Down the Bones* by Natalie Goldberg
- *How to Write Science Fiction & Fantasy* by Orson Scott Card
- *Courage & Craft: Writing You Life Into Story* by Barbara Abercrombie
- *Writing Successful Self-Help & How-To Books* by Jean Marie Stine
- *Getting Started as a Freelance Write* by Robert W. Bly
- *How to Get Happily Publisher* by Judith Appelbaun
- *Pen On Fire* by Barbara Demarco-Barrett
- *How to Write & Sell Simple Information For Fun and Profit* by Bob Bly
- *On Writing* by Stephen King
- *Write & Get Paid* by Anthony Tinsman

- *James A. Michener's Writers Handbook*
- *The Writer's Legal Guide* by Tad Crawford and Kay Murray
- *Business and Legal Forms for Authors and Self-Publishers* by Tad Crawford

10 Magazines For the Writer in Prison

Here are some magazines that you may want to subscribe to? They can supply you with a lot of inspiration and tips. You can
get some of them from the discount magazine services.

1. *Writer's Digest*
2. *The Writer*
3. *Poet & Writer's*
4. *The Writers Journal*
5. *The Editorial Eye*
6. *Byline*
7. *Children's Book Insider*
8. *Locus* (sci-fi writing)
9. *The Horror Writer*
10. *Authorship* (magazine article writing)

A Final Thought

More prisoners have used writing to get money over any other strategy I have ever seen. Every prison commissary that I know of sells pen and paper and envelopes. How you use those weapons of mass communication is up to you.

THE MILLIONAIRE PRISONER: PART 3

"All I need is a sheet of paper and something to write with, and then I can turn the world upside down."

– Friedrich Nietzshe

Helpful Information for New Writers:
Please print and send to your incarcerated writers interested in sending in submissions.

Hello New Writers!

I am a former television journalist with decades of experience working for CBS News, CNN, OBS and CNBC. I developed an interest in prison reform while producing documentaries about crime for CBS's show 48 Hours. Michael Hiestand is a former columnist for USA TODAY who has written for many national publications. And we have a handful of New York University college students helping out as well.

We started Prison Writers because we all believe a crucial voice is missing in the prison reform debate – the voice of the people who live behind bars. Our mission is twofold. One, we want to build wider awareness of what it's like to live in prison, for people on the outside. The more people know about the realities of prison, the more people who'll believe in prison reform. And two, we're giving people who live on the inside a chance to be heard, a chance to be part of the national dialogue on reforming prisons. What happens in prison doesn't stay in prison – anymore. We want to get the truth OUT.

But there's more to it than that. The better writer someone is, the more doors that will open up for him or her. We all have millions of ideas in our heads, but they're not worth much if we can't express them in a way that makes people listen. And writing is the best way to practice that; you learn to organize your thoughts and get them in the right order, you learn when to add colorful examples or personal touches and, with practice, you learn how to say more with less words. The better you get at putting your own thoughts into words, the more confident you'll feel about yourself in your future.

And along the way, we think you will start to feel part of a bigger community – the Prison Writers Family. You'll also learn how to meet deadlines and set goals and expectations for yourself that you can meet. And that, my friends, is how we think we can help you the most. That's the real reason we started PrisonWriters.com – for you guys.

So, what to write about?

We're interested in personal stories about something that happened to you in prison or that you witnessed firsthand. Let's leave the research-based reporting to the academics and the policy experts. We'd much rather you wrote about what you know, because only you – as an incarcerated individual living it – can offer the authentic points of view that people in the outside don't have and never will, without hearing from you.

Getting Started:

If someone asks you to think of five things that happened to you in prison that you'll never forget ... what would they be? If you think it makes a good story about prison, consider writing a story about it. It could be something horrible and shameful (that sheds light on the violence in prison) or it could be something hilarious and bizarre that could only happen in prison. How about telling us one of those stories?

THE MILLIONAIRE PRISONER: PART 3

The best way to start is with an <u>amazing story that really happened to you or in front of you in prison</u>. Write a STORY that's 500-2000 words in length – preferably typed – with a beginning, middle and end. Your writing can be serious, funny or straightforward as long as it's grounded in truth.

Topics:
The list below should give you an idea of the kinds of topics we're looking for... do you have any personal stories that illustrate any of these topics?

- Any funny stories about something weird, bizarre or amusing that has happened in prison.
- How gangs operate in the various presidents you've been in.
- Stories about corruption, theft, abuse or smuggling involving prison staff.
- How prisons create better criminals instead of rehabilitating them.
- What you would change about prison if you were in charge – and why?

How a person program, class or course has helped or changed you – and why?

<u>Extra bonus points for this one! Anything you can write about your crime (assuming you committed one) starting with details of the crime that occur, what led up to it, regrets, your victims, how you feel about it now – anything.</u>

What Not To Write About:
- The intricate details of your particular case or an explanation of your innocence.

- Something someone else told you about or that you heard second-hand.
- A rant about all the reasons you hate being in prison.
- A rambling essay about a bunch of different things that don't tie together.

Tips:
- Write about something that really happened to you or that you witnessed first-hand.
- We're not looking for "model prisoners" stories. We're looking for authentic and real. So if the truth is messy, violent or unflattering – don't bother sugarcoating it.
- Include enough visual details so the reader feels like he's almost there watching it.
- No previously published stories will be considered.
- And our apologies, but we're not accepting poetry OR FICTION at this time.

If you hand write your story, please make the writing easy to read. Avoid tiny handwriting or hard-to-read handwriting.
Show vs. Tell: let's say you want to write about how prisons teach incarcerated people to be better criminals instead of rehabilitating them. Rather than just telling us that in a general way, think of a true story that describes one particular prisoner or situation or event or day or conversation that you think shows us.
Important Notes:

- If we like your submission, will be back in touch with editing suggestions – or, if it's good enough to publish, will send you your payment ($10) for publishing it!

- Don't forget to write your name on your story! No pen names or anonymous authors allowed!
- Also, include the address you'd like us to send your payment, if we accept one of your submissions.
- Payment will be in the form of a money order, so send us the name of a friend or family member if you're not allowed to receive money orders.
- Please include a short bio and a photo with your next letter in case we accept your submission.
- Photos will not be returned unless specifically requested.
- Writing submissions will not be returned unless specifically requested and if a SASE is included.

Send stories to: New Writer
Prison Writers
PO Box 1430
New York, NY 10276

Thanks for your time and good luck!
Cheers!
Loen Kelley
The Prison Writers Team

CHAPTER TWELVE

Marketing Mastery

"A man is rich in proportion to the number of things he can afford to let alone."

– Henry David Thoreau

One of the best definitions of marketing I have ever read is in Dan S. Kennedy's *The Ultimate Marketing Plan, 4th Edition:*
"Getting the right message to the right people via the right media and methods – effectively, efficiently, and profitably."

I do not have enough space in this chapter to show you all the tactics you can use to do what Dan Kennedy defined. And I already wrote about marketing in *The Millionaire Prisoner, Part 2*. But I do want to share some of the things I've learned since I wrote *TMP*.

Your Target Audience

In *TMP* I asked several questions to help identify your target audience. Since I wrote that I've had the opportunity to study the stratagems of marketing gurus Dan Kennedy and Perry Marshall. They helped me understand that I left off the most important question we should ask before we set out to market our products or services:

THE MILLIONAIRE PRISONER: PART 3

Does this market have money and the authority to spend it?

Think about that question for a minute. Look at my target audience – prisoners. How many prisoners have money? Not many. So, this may not be a good market? It depends on what your goals are. Why not find another market where they have money to spend? It takes the same energy to market to a rich business owner as it does to a prisoner. So, spend your energy where you'll get the most return.

The second part of that question is do they have the authority to spend the money. Some doctors have money for their health care services available. But the board or administrator controls the purse strings. Sending them your marketing materials would be futile unless they can actually spend the money. Of course, they have their own personal income to spend. That could make them a possible target audience? Once you find the right market who has money to spend, and the authority to spend it, you have to get your message in front of them. And they have to repeatedly see it. If you can learn how to do this correctly, you'll never go hungry.

Online Marketing and Advertising

It's 2021 as I write this. If I ask 10 people what I should do to market this book, most will say some form of online marketing. Especially on Amazon. It's a fact of life that big tech (Amazon, Facebook, Google, etc.) controls a big piece of the world as we know it. And most shoppers online always check in with Amazon. Especially for books. But I'm old enough to remember a world with no Internet. I grew up in the 1980s. My grandparents owned an antique store and they could not market online because there was no Internet then. There is now. So, you should always look to see how you can market your products and services online.

That doesn't mean you should automatically pay for online ads. You need to first determine where your target audience hangs out. Can you reach them for free? Are there Facebook groups for your target audience? Other chat rooms? Does your product or service fit in with other products being promoted on the website? Are you ready to fill the back end of things after they order? Because that's a part of marketing also. Your whole process speaks loudly. You think about this 24/7! Or you should. Here's some more tips.

<u>Always do your research first!</u> Use online groups and social media to find out what your customers pain points are. What language do they use? That's how you find the *right message* to send them. That's how you find the number one keyword to advertise with. It's all about your research. Dr. Glenn Livingston is an expert at this type of research and has free resources online to help you learn how to do it. See www.glennlivingston.com/AD.php.

<u>Build your own platform</u>. If you only have a Facebook or Twitter account/page that you market through, you're at risk. Just ask Donald Trump. You need a processing platform that you own and control. The best platform would be your own website with the regularly updated repeat customer/client database. It should have names, snail mail an email addresses, and phone numbers. Then you could create your own newsletter or magazine and services just for them. That way you don't lose 73 million followers if Big Tech decides they don't like what you're saying.

Create more content. The best marketing strategy is more! More books. More songs. More products. More services. Think about the rappers who dropped several albums during the pandemic. Or the authors who dropped several books each year. These are the people who make millions. How can you do this in your own business? Put out more quality stuff catered to your target audience. Then watch the money pile up.

Automate your marketing. If someone clicks on your online ad, everything that happens next should be automated. That way you can spend your time on the things that really matter. Like writing successful sales material and ads. Or fulfilling orders. There are programs and systems online that can help you do this. Infusionsoft is one. Most email programs have autoresponders you can use for free. Set it and forget it!

Test, fail fast, and test again. No matter where you place your ads you need to test them. Then tweak them. And test them again to get better results. You can do this a lot easier with online ads. Sometimes one word changed can bring a better response. But you'll never know unless you try. Don't test a whole new ad at first. Just try out little changes one at a time. Compare results. Keep what works, throw out what doesn't. Keep testing and make your ads better.

"The secret to everything is split testing."
– Perry Marshall

These are just a few tips. I've listed some great resources at the end of this chapter that you should get and study.

Day of the Dozens

On my tablet newsfeed was an article about Krispy Kreme® doing a "Day of the Dozens" marketing ploy. It was the 12th day of the 12th month of the year, or December 12th. So, you could walk into one of their stores and get 12 Donuts for $1.00 on December 12. I liked that idea and wondered how we can use it? Here's how.

On December 12th of every year, plan out your "Marketing Dozen." Or the 12 things you want to implement in the next year. Get a piece of paper and write Marketing Dozen at the top. Then number your list 1-12 of things you want to implement. Here's an example of how it can be done:

2021 Marketing Design

1. Write sales letter to new target audience.
2. Test Google Adwords campaign.
3. Obtain at least six testimonials to use in print ads.
4. Set up a customer newsletter.
5. Create better unique selling propositions for each product.
6. Send out press releases.
7. Start a referral rewards program.
8. Test Amazon advertising campaign.
9. Set up social media pages and automate updates.
10. Write guest blog post for industry influencers.
11. Redo your website.
12. Do a video sales letter (VSL) or short-form infomercial.

Another lesson in this example is to borrow good ideas when you see them. You don't have to make and sell donuts to benefit from the "Day of the Dozens". But you do have to take action and implement some of the steps on your marketing dozen. Do one a week. Or one a month. In no time you'll have more customers than you could ever dream of.

Writing Advertisements

I subscribe to *Prison Legal News* and *Kite* magazine. Both cater to the prisoner audience. Because I'm a cellpreneur I always read every ad in both publications. Guess what? 98% of the businesses who advertise in these magazines get it wrong. They could either do it better, don't do it long enough, or just plain do it wrong. I guess they don't like making money? Or they have plenty of customers and are satisfied? OK, I'll stop making jokes. The plain truth is that most of them don't know how to do it right. Placing an ad in a publication has a science behind it. If you have a GTL Tablet, just run a search for the audio book *Scientific Advertising* by Claude Hopkins. That's where your education should start. I'll give you some more books at the end of this chapter you should get and study. But here are some mistakes these companies make:

- They have no customer testimonials in their ads;
- They don't create urgency with a time limited special offer or other device;
- They don't list their complete contact info;
- They don't track their ads (if it's the only ad you're running that's different);
- They don't offer a money-back guarantee;
- They don't use photos of the product.

These are just some of the mistakes companies make. If you're going to spend your own money placing ads then you should learn how to write great ads. This goes for placing ads online as well.

Your Personal Swipe File

One of the best pieces of advice I ever read is to create your own "swipe file". A swipe file is a file folder filled with ads that make you want to act or buy the product. These could be classified ads, half page ads, full page ads, envelope teasers, direct mail pieces, and/or photo layouts. You keep these files so that you can steal from them when writing your own ads.

I have a huge folder filled with full-page ads out of magazines. Not just ads for books either. Lawyer's ads. Supplement and vitamin ads. Sleep number bed ads. All kinds of them from different markets aimed at assorted audiences. That's how you learn and get better. By adapting other ideas from outside your comfort zone. You don't have to go to school to learn how to do it right. But you do have to study. Learn from the masters. You can start by creating your own swipe file.

Recommended Reading

You can get a world class education into marketing like a master in the following books:

- *The Ultimate Marketing Plan, 4th Edition* by Dan S. Kennedy
- *Magnetic Marketing* by Dan S. Kennedy

- *No B.S. Direct Marketing for Non-Direct Marketing Businesses* by Dan S. Kennedy
- *Ultimate Guide to Google Adwords* by Parry Marshall, Mike Rhodes & Bryan Todd
- *Ultimate Guide to Facebook Advertising* by Perry Marshall, Keith Krance & Thomas Meloche
- *Ultimate Guide to Amazon Advertising* by Timothy P. Seward
- *Facebook Marketing: An Hour A Day* by Mari Smith
- *80/20 Sales and Marketing* by Perry Marshall
- *No B.S. Trust-Based Marketing* by Dan S. Kennedy & Matt Zagula
- *The Advertising Solution* by Craig Simpson with Brian Kurtz
- *Scientific Advertising* by Claude Hopkins
- *Tested Advertising Methods* by John Caples
- *Breakthrough Advertising* by Eugene Schwartz
- *Ca$h Copy* by Dr. Jeffrey Lant
- <u>Recommended Listening</u>
- If you have a GTL Tablet you can listen to the following to get more tips, tactics, and strategies:
- *My Life In Advertising* by Claude Hopkins
- Online Email Marketing
- Internet Marketing Strategies
- Mega Nasty Rich
- Mobile Marketing & Social Media For Small Business
- How to Get Targeted Traffic On the Internet Now!
- Social Media Men Podcast

In the next chapter I'll show you some additional promotional tactics.

CHAPTER THIRTEEN

How to Walk On Clouds by Using Videos
"When it comes to marketing online, the most powerful form of content is videos."
– Thomas Meloche

There's a lot of talk about using videos to demonstrate online. In *The Copywriter's Handbook, 4th Edition*, Robert Bly writes: "Video is taking over marketing and the world. According to a study by Cisco, a 2019 video will have accounted for up to 80% of all online traffic. And consumers are 85% more likely to buy your product after viewing your video." Because it's so important I'll share with you some secrets that I gleaned from the top video experts. But first we'll deal with how some prisoners, and former prisoners, are using video to succeed.

Prison Lifestyle Video Succe$$

Some prisoners have had their 15 minutes of fame because of their videos going viral. Omar Broadway shot some raw prison footage on a contraband cell phone. HBO picked up that video and turned it into a whole show. Other prisoners have used crowdfunding campaigns to get money. The best ones are those that have videos. Of course, we can't talk about videos without talking about YouTube.

THE MILLIONAIRE PRISONER: PART 3

The publishing gods have a funny way of showing us writer's things. As I was putting the finishing touches on this chapter, I got the July 2020 *Prison Legal News* in the mail. Anthony Accurso wrote an article titled "The Popularity of YouTube Prison Lifestyle Videos." He detailed how Joe Guerrero has 1.2 million YouTube subscribers to his *After Prison Show*. After 700 videos, which started out as grainy amateurish vlogs (video + blog = vlog), he now earns six-figures as a social media influencer. His most popular video about how to make a tattoo gun got 2.3 million views. Christina Randall is a former prisoner that has 400,000 subscribers to her YouTube channel and most of them are women. Marcus "Big Here" Timmons has become a social media star based off his videos and now makes a living speaking. People have always been, and always will be, fascinated by prisons life and culture. Think how well MSNBC's *Lock Up*, We channel's *Love After Lockup*, and C&I's *The Big House* do.

At the end of King Guru's *Pretty Girls Love Bad Boys* he says this: "If you can get someone to go on Facebook, Snapchat, or Instagram, look us up! Maybe once you see the blogs and pictures of how we're really living inside of these level 4 prisons then you'll know for yourself that everything that comes from The Cell Block is authentic. Maybe that's what it'll take for some of you to wholeheartedly follow our advice and finally start getting everything life has to offer." The key to what he said is "vlogs". Like other prisoners you can start with You Tube.

Steve Stockman is a writer and director of short films, commercials, music videos, and TV shows. He wrote and directed the award-winning 2007 MGM feature film *Two Weeks*, starring Sally Field and Ben Chaplin. His website is stevestockman.com. Here's what he says about video in his great book, *How To Shoot Video That Doesn't Suck*:

"Great video is a communication tool of unparalleled impact. It can change history, inspire movements, share and amplify emotions, and build community. Bad video is turned off. Nobody watches a bad video. Not your employee, even if you tell them to. Not your parents, even if you send them 'the cutest' videos of your kids."

With all this in mind, how can a prisoner use video? Here are some ideas:

- Sell your books or arts and crafts products.
- Post a video of yourself on penpal and dating sites to get more hits.
- Start a prison blog and discuss up-to-date topics dealing with prison politics, reform, and culture.
- Have other people give you testimonials and videos that support your expertise or product.
- Use it as a supplement to an application or resumé.

These are just some ideas. The sky is the limit. Just because you don't have lots of money doesn't mean you should skip this avenue of success. Not if you want to stand out. Even if you have to start by having a family member or friend record your video visit and then post it online? Or having said family member, friend, or client/customer post a video to Facebook as a testimonial about you? Videos can change the game for you.

THE MILLIONAIRE PRISONER: PART 3

> *"You'll still be posting photos and writing posts, but nothing builds trust and value more than video."*
> – Keith Krance, founder of Dominate Web Media

That's the evolution that I hope you get after reading this book. As I write this, it's the middle of 2020, so think in terms of 2020 technology and beyond. How can you use it to achieve your dreams? So begin to think outside the box you're living in and start using videos to showcase your most important product – you! (BTW, *Pretty Girls Love Bad Boys* by King Guru is highly recommended for every prisoner who wants to get girls, or keep the one you already got). The rest of this chapter will show you how to make better videos.

How To Make Videos That Get Viewed

The best videos entertain the audience. They offer intrigue. Leaving the audience seeking more, and wanting to know what happens next. So, the first key to video success is to know who your audience is? To make the best video ask yourself the following questions:

- Who is your target audience? Is it a possible pen pal? Is it a potential customer? Who is it?
- What is your intention? What do you want the video to accomplish?
- What is your competition doing? Are they using videos? Can you learn from them?

Answer these questions and put yourself in your viewer's place. Try to imagine what they'll feel when they watch your video. Once you know who you're making your video for an what you want to accomplish then it's time to make your video. There will be four types of videos that you primarily use for cellpreneurial success. They are promotional videos, how-to videos, an interview video, and a video testimonial. Each has its own rules of the best practices. As Steve Stockman says, "the most memorable home videos and documentaries tell stories. Those stories don't just magically appear in the edit room. You have to imagine them before you start shooting." So, what's the story you're trying to tell?

The Video Interview

I've put this one first because it's something a prisoner could do. Have your family member friend record your interview through a video visit. Prepare ahead of time what you want them to ask you and what you'll say. Both of you should be relaxed and go with the flow. If both of you trust each other the interview will be better. Don't look at the screen or yourself in the corner of the screen. Look at the camera lens when answering questions. That way you'll be looking directly at the person watching your interview.

If it's the other way around and you're conducting an interview, think about the following things. Think background. Because it matters. For instance, if they are an artist, have them sit in their studio. Are they an author? Have them sit in a library or with books behind them. Don't have them sit where people will be walking behind them. They are not a newscaster. Watch good documentaries on TV and see how the backgrounds are carefully chosen to fit the image of the person being interviewed. Remember, it's all about the story you're trying to tell, even in a video interview.

The Promotional Video

What are you trying to promote? Who is it for? Do they already know you? Or is it the first time they are meeting you? Try to think about your target audience (or your customer/client's) needs. Build a relationship with the viewer, not a sale. If you're selling a product or service, use a video sales letter (VSL). More on those in a minute. If you're promoting something it's best to have testimonials.

The Video Testimonial

I love watching late night/early morning infomercials. Not because I can buy from them. I never have. I watch them to learn tricks that I might be able to use in my own marketing. Especially now that I've studied video making. The best infomercials use testimonials. There's a long-form infomercial on right now where Larry King interviews a "credit secrets" book author. It uses lots of testimonials. We know it works because they keep running it over and over again. I would love to be able to do that for my books and play them on the institution channels of many prisons across America. If you can use a video testimonial of success stories of your customers/clients you'll sell more products/services.

The How-To Video

Explain only one thing per video. Think Joe Guerrero's 2.3-million-viewed how-to-make-a-prison-tattoo-gun video. It's about one topic. Show your audience. Think "show and tell" from grade school. Don't get distracted and off topic. If it doesn't pertain to the topic of the video, it shouldn't be in the video. When explaining things, try not to use jargon or long convoluted sentences. Do it like you were explaining and showing it to a kid.

The Video Sales Letter (VSL)

Video Sales Letters (VSLs) are used in several different ways. They can be used on the home page to sell what you want visitors to your website to do. These are typically short 2-3 minutes or less in length. If it's a business to business (B2B) home page video it can be a little longer (4 minutes), but not too much longer. VSLs can also be used on second level pages on your website. These videos are longer, typically 5-7 minutes. Lastly, there are long form VSLs. These run anywhere from 15-45 minutes. When thinking about time and length of your videos, use your TV as a gauge of what's proper.

TV commercials are normally 30-second stories. Network hour is 44 minutes long. That leaves time for the network to put in commercial breaks. A movie trailer is normally 2 1/2 minutes long. Informercials are either 30 minutes or 1 hour long. Here's how you can compute those numbers in words when you write your VSL script. Normally, it's 120 words per minute. So, a 30-second commercial will have 60 words. There can be more if the speaker talks rapidly. A 10-minute script would have 1,200 words. A 45-minute script would have 7,000 words. Once you write out your script you can use a voice-over estimate to see how long it will be. Upload your script at:

THE MILLIONAIRE PRISONER: PART 3

https://www.thevoicerealm.com/count-script.php

9 Rules For Creating An Effective VSL

When creating a VSL you are marketing. Someone has to write the script. Here are master copywriter Robert Bly's nine rules for creating an effective VSL. You can find these in his book, *The Copywriter's Handbook, 4th Edition:*

1. Grab the audience's attention.
2. Tell an engaging story.
3. Keep it simple.
4. Use short sentences and short words. No words with more than 9 letters.
5. Use short paragraphs of only 2 or 3 sentences.
6. If you have to prove a claim or fact, do it by inserting a chart or graph.
7. Explain the solution within the first minute or two.
8. Don't use more than two numbers in each sentence.
9. Use a positive and enthusiastic voice. But it should also sound authoritative.

Your opening should be simple. If I was to do a VSL, here's what my opening could be:

"Hi, I'm Josh Kruger for Carceral Wealth, and today, we'll show you how you can help make your loved one's prison stay easier and better than ever before."

A simple closing to my VSL could be this:

"So, if you want to see what Carceral Wealth can do for you and your loved one, give us a call right away at xxx-xxx-xxxx. We'll give you a free estimate. Want to contact us for more info? Visit www.millionaireprisoner.com and sign up today. We can't wait to help you make your loved one's prison stay a whole lot better. Call now or send us a message today!"

How To Walk On Clouds By Using Videos

Richard Clayman is the owner and founder of Cloudwalker Videoworks. He has 25 years' experience as a Hollywood producer, director, writer, and executive. He also spent a decade teaching at top film schools such as the University of Southern California School of Cinematic Arts. Now he uses all that to write, produce, and direct videos for law firms, finance and insurance companies, non-profits, multi-million-dollar corporations, and municipalities. As a "filmmaker in a sea of videographers," Richard is a seminal voice in the industry. You can learn more at http://www.cloudwalkerfilms.com. Here's what he says:

"Excluding their potential to drive traffic to your site, videos on your website are designed for one of three purposes:

1. To serve as a first meeting
2. To demonstrate expertise
3. To sell a particular service or clarify an arcane offering

The most compelling videos have the person looking at the camera and telling us more about who he or she is rather than what he or she does. This could be the CEO, COO, CFO, managing partner, or, in the case of bio page videos, an individual. Ideally these are 1:00 minute videos for Home page, Services page, and About Us page. For certain industries, testimonial page videos with happy clients complete the job of engendering trust. Don't forget – website visitors don't get there by accident. They know what you do. Their unarticulated need is to know who you are, in the context of what you do. The result? Your first meetings will be more like second meetings, because the potential client has already decided not on your firm, but on you.

Expertise is often shown through periodic blog or newsletter videos. These can take the form of mock interviews, panel discussions, or, simply, one person speaking directly to the camera. It is most cost efficient to pan out several of these – e.g., 15 pieces for weekly distribution – so they can be shot in a single day. You can have a film professional work with you to set up a mini studio at your office and show you how to do simple edits and makeup. In that way, you can address timely issues quickly without the cost of bringing in a professional crew. The result won't be at the highest level, but, for this type of piece, will suffice.

Service providers have a particular product they would like to push to existing clients or referral sources, such as a certain kind of trust vehicle for estate planning and asset protection purposes. In addition, some businesses require a quick clarification on their mechanisms in value propositions. These needs are best satisfied through vibrant, energetic animation. This is a longer process than live action videos, but, generally, takes no more than a couple of months to complete.

It would be nice to be able to do any of these videos on your own or hire your nephew, the film student. This is always a mistake. We all know that everyone has a very deep and personal relationship with TV and film. When something is wrong in writing, performance, makeup, framing, sound, location, music, logo animation – any number of pitfalls - the visitor will know it and immediately ascribe the discomfort in viewing it to your level of professionalism and taste. Not good.

As in anything else of importance, make sure you hire the best.

On the other hand, if all of those items are accomplished at a top level, the visitor will also recognize that, and you will immediately stand above your competition (and most others they encounter on the Internet.)

So, make sure you hire a real professional filmmaker to do your videos and you'll get the best possible result."

Most of us won't be able to hire a professional right away. So, here's some technical stuff you can utilize when making videos. Rick Gee of www.MarketingProfitStrategiesBlog.com says that all you need is a flip-video camera or a Kodak Zi8 pocket camcorder. That Kodak HD camcorder is less than $200 brand new. And if you use YouTube you can edit your videos for free using YouTube's own free editing software. The best YouTube videos are about 3 minutes long and funny. Great YouTube video experts to study are James Wedmore, Andy Jenkins, and Mike Stewart.

Some other video editing software is:
 Windows 10 Video Editor Program
 Adobe Premiere Pro
 Apple Final Cut Pro X
 Adobe Premier Elements (for beginners)

Whoever is shooting the video needs to do the following. Turn off the "zoom" feature. Don't use it. Instead, set the lens all the way wide and move closer to what you're filming. And don't ever use "digital zoom". Matter of fact, turn off all of your camera's digital features. Keep the light at your back. Remember to think about your background. Also, use the "rule of thirds" doctrine when shooting video of something standing (or sitting) still. This means they should be off to the left or right of the center of the shot. In a third of the screen. If you've ever watched "American Greed" on CNBC, they do this perfectly. Try to use external microphones like booms or clip-on mics. If you or your loved one is going to be a regular vlogger using a webcam they need a clip on mic. Those cost less than $25 at stores like Best Buy®. And remember to tell them to look at the camera not the screen!

Edit, edit, and edit your videos. Make them short and memorable. So, edit what doesn't work. The mantra is "when in doubt, cut it out." Turn off the computer's transition effects before you start editing. When you first start, your videos won't be the best. Joe Guerrero's videos started out as homemade, grainy mishaps. Now, after 700 videos, he's an expert. Just remember that no video is better than a bad video. You only get one chance to make a good first impression.

If you want more help, check out www.TheVideoMarketing-Guru.com. You can also post your videos on Vimeo.com. It's free. You can post your videos across many other platforms through Traffic Geyser (http://trafficgeyser.com). But you'll have to pay a fee.

If you have a tablet (I have a GTL Inspire™), see if they got *How To Make Money With Online Videos* or *Optimizing Your Videos For Free Traffic*. Listen to those.

If you're serious about making videos, then you need to read Steve Stockman's book *How To Shoot Videos That Don't Suck*. A final word from Steve:

"Art – and video is an art – requires passion. It requires emotion. It requires commitment and a willingness to get up and do what's in your heart, regardless of what others will say. It's hard, and if everyone could do it, there would never be a non-hit song or a non-bestselling book. Studios would never release a bad movie, and every video on YouTube would have the same huge number of hits."

But just because it's hard doesn't mean you can't do it. Millionaire Prisoners do what unsuccessful prisoners won't do. To go to the next level and rise above the masses you can use videos. That's how you can walk on clouds from a prison cell.

CHAPTER FOURTEEN

Publicity – PR

"If you're not gonna go all the way, why go at all?"
– Joe Nathan

PR = Public Relations. Millionaire businessman Ted Nicholas defined it as the "means of using the media to help get your message out to the public." Most experts will tell you that getting your name in the media can do wonders for your career. But you can't just get your name mentioned once. No, you need to consistently have your name (or product) show up as the go-to expert on your chosen topic. In this chapter I'll give you some ideas of how you can do that.

Getting your name or product mentioned in the press is great. It does three things:

1. Allows you to reach your target audience; and
2. Allows you to utilize media leverage to build authority; and
3. Allows you to pull in new customers or clients.

These benefits will bring in quality leads and sales if you have your lead magnet and sales funnel set up to convert prospects. How do you get this media attention? You can do it yourself, or you can work with a PR firm. PR experts charge upwards of thousands of dollars a month. Most of us don't have that kind of money to throw away. So, you're going to have to do it yourself. Yes, it will be work, but it will be worth it.

Your Target Audience

Because you don't have the time (or the money) to approach every media outlet you need to first define your target audience. Once you find them, you'll know how to reach them. For instance, my readers are prisoners. All media is not equal when reaching prisoners. *Prison Legal News* and *Kite* magazine will be better for me than *Cosmopolitan* and *USA Today*. So, who is your target audience? What magazines do they read? What radio shows do they listen to? What television shows do they watch? What websites do they visit? Don't know? Find out. Or else you'll just waste your time and money getting publicity that doesn't pay off.

In his book *How To Make Millions With Your Ideas*, marketing master Dan S. Kennedy says these are "The 5 P's of Publicity":

1. Be Predictive.
2. Be Proactive.
3. Be Public (mainstream).
4. Be a Personality.
5. Be Persistent.

> "*Media choices must be strategic and situational, factoring in your target clientele, their preferred means of being made aware of and interested in new ideas, information, products and services, their trust*

triggers, as well as a measurable return on investment."

–Dan S. Kennedy

15 Common Mistakes Entrepreneurs Make

Pam Lantos is a publicity expert and author of *Don't Tell Me It's Impossible Until After I've Already Done It*. She's also co-author of *I See Your Name Everywhere*. She says that most people don't know how to get publicity and that they make 15 common mistakes. They are:

1. They think that hundreds of customers will come from one hit.
2. They are not unique in their approach.
3. They think they can't get into a large publication.
4. They think small publications don't matter.
5. They think their ideas are wonderful.
6. They pitch themselves instead of a story idea.
7. They pitch to the wrong person.
8. They don't find out what reporters, producers and editors really want.
9. They don't answer to the reporter's questions.
10. They don't get straight to the point.
11. They don't respect the reporter's time.
12. They don't gear their pitches to the specific publication.
13. They make their pitch an advertisement for their products or services.
14. They don't understand the importance of frequency of publicity.

15. They don't provide their publicist with material and information in a timely manner.

For a free publicity consultation with Pam send her an email at Pam@prpr.net. Her free newsletter *PR/PR Pulse!* Is also available on her website, www.prpr.net.
Another good source of information is Joan Stewart (www.publicity-hound.com) and her *The Publicity Hound's Tips of the Week* free ezine.

Millionaire Prisoner PR Tips

Every day Dr. Jeffrey Lant started his day by contacting at least 5 media sources. He became a multimillionaire from his how-to books in consulting business. When he was still inside, federal prisoner Michael Santos made sure every day that mail was picked up, there was one letter in there reaching out to someone new. He became a millionaire after he was released. Notice the similarities? Each and every day they took action. What are you doing daily to get publicity? Here's what you should be doing.

• Collect reporters and other media contact information. Remember how to do this from the networking chapter? If you don't want to take the time to acquire these names, emails, and addresses yourself you can always buy lists. Two of the best are:
  • Cision's database (http://us.cision.com/index.asp)
  • Gebbie Press (http://gebbiepress.com)
• Once you find news media people in your market, follow them on social media, especially Twitter.

- Sign up for Help a Reporter Out (HARO). It's free at http://helpareporter.com. A paid service can be found at http://profnet.com.
- Set up Google Alerts (http://alerts.google.com). Sign up so that you're notified each time someone mentions your name, your websites URLs, your book titles, your competitors, your industry statistics, blogging news of your industry. When other people mention you or your products, reach out to them.
- Do podcast tours by phone. They now have podcasts on the GTL Tablets. Listen to them and see how you can tailor your pitch to possibly be interviewed on them? Or start your own podcast.
- Do blog tours. Guest-post articles on blogs that your target audience reads. Repost their content on your blog or social media pages. Share.
- Do pre-PR and post-PR. Pre-PR would announce a new book, product, etc. Post-PR would highlight an interview, video clip, etc. For instance, let's say you signed a deal with Mike Enemigo to publish one of your books? You should do a press release announcing you signing that deal with Mike. Then do another one once the book comes out. Then another one once your book is mentioned in *Prison Legal News* or *Kite* magazine.
- Once you start getting media mentions you need to show that off in your marketing materials and on your website/social media pages. At the top of your website, you should have a "As Seen In/On" logos of media outlets as soon as you get them. This adds credibility and authority.
- Don't forget radio shows. People still listen to the radio. You can sign up for the free service Radio Guest List (www.radioguestlist.com). Just remember that when you go

on someone else's radio show to answer questions quickly by getting straight to the point. Talk to the host in sound bites. Be a great guest so they have you back.

These are just some tips to remember when seeking publicity. PR is not selling. It's better used to get credibility and establish your name as the expert. That way when people seek out someone in your industry your name will be who they think first!

The Brass Check

- If you've never had the opportunity to read Ryan Holiday's books you're missing out. He's a marketing expert and had the opportunity to apprentice with Robert Greene (*48 Laws of Power*). I especially love Holidays books *Trust Me, I'm Lying* and *Perennial Seller*. Here are two ideas I've borrowed from him and altered for us prisoners:
- Newsjack your way into conversations online. What's trending? Write an article or blog post slanted at what all the news media is talking about. But in a way that puts the story back on you. Currently, as I write this, the protests and riots over racial inequality and George Floyd's death at the hands of the police is all over every news outlet. A prisoner could write about the racial inequality problem in prisons as its own powder keg waiting to explode. For more about how to do this type of PR/marketing, read *Newsjacking* by David Meerman Scott.
- If you're an artist, author, or have created a business or something to sell, then you could do something like this next tactic to get some publicity. Put up a small billboard ad on a main road coming into your hometown. It could say

something like this: "Thank you _____ County, you sent me away to rot in a prison cell. Look at me now!" On the Billboard you have your photo and website (or Facebook address). On the day it goes up, you have someone take a photo of it and send it to all the local newspapers, radio and TV stations. With the photo you say, "I find it outrageous that a convicted murderer (or whatever you are) can put up an outlandish, offensive billboard in this County." Ryan Holiday says to make it come from "a concerned citizen" and that it made their daughter cry. Lbvs. Brilliant. Once the newspaper or TV station runs with it you post that clip or article everywhere. Stunt marketing 101! Just remember that you're not trying to sell product from the billboard, just to get publicity that you can use to get more publicity. To get your name out there. Or back out there. Fame is in the name!

20 Ways To Get Publicity From Media Outlets

Here are some ways that many successful businesses use to get publicity:

1.	Radio	12.	Magazines
2.	Podcasts	13.	Catalogs
3.	TV	14.	Online Videos
4.	Online	15.	Press Releases
5.	Search Engines	16.	Books
6.	Ezines	17.	Trade Shows
7.	Email	18.	Blogs
8.	Online Advertising	19.	Newspapers
9.	Postcards	20.	Telephone
10.	Direct Mail	21.	Seminars
11.	Social Media		

You can't do all of the above. Especially not from a cell. So pick three of them. Master one of those three. Then do the other two. If you do that, you'll run circles around your competitors. Especially your fellow prisoners.

Holiday Promotions

Every month there is some kind of event/special day that you could use to tie-in and promote you, your business, and or product. Here's a simple version:

January = New Year's Day
February = Valentine's Day
March = St. Patrick's Day
April = Easter
May = Mother's Day
June = Father's Day
July = Fourth of July
August = Back-to-school
September = Labor Day
October = Halloween
November = Thanksgiving
December = Christmas

Chase Calendar of Events is a huge book ($70+) that will give you a whole bunch of events/celebrations for every day/week/month of the year. If you're serious about getting publicity you need to learn how to use these days/events that people are already celebrating.

Your Media Press Kit

To take advantage of all the media exposure you want to get you need a Press Kit. It should have its own section on your website and should consist of the following:

1. Biography is about you. You should have four different ones of varying lengths:
   - 2 Lines (120 characters)
   - Short Bio (50 words)
   - Medium Bio (100 words)
   - Long Bio (400 to 600 words)
2. All of your press releases. Have them listed in order of the latest, most up-to-date to the oldest.
3. Publicity photos. Try to offer different photos, and photos of your books, products, etc. Have at least one professional photo of yourself.
4. Have sample interview questions, tip sheets, quotes and videos/sound bites.
5. Free articles that people can use as is. Make sure you have a variety and length available for use in different formats.
6. Constantly update your media materials on your website as you create new materials.

Lastly, write articles for relevant publications that reach you target audience. Provide relevant tips that can help them. Always have a call to action at the end of your article enticing the reader to continue the conversation further. Never stop seeking out new outlets to get free publicity!

Recommended Reading

For more about how to get publicity in this day and age I encourage you to get, read, study, and master the following:

- *The New Rules for Marketing and PR* by David Meerman Scott

CHAPTER FIFTEEN

6 P's of Sustainable Business Growth
"Set up a business system that makes money no matter what you do."
– MJ DeMarco

The 6 P's of Sustainable Business Growth

Do you remember the "P90X" workout craze? I do. A lot of prisoners I know had the books and were doing it. What a great name though – P90X. Easy to remember and different. Well, business consultant and strategist Jason Ciment (www.GetVisible.Com) came up with the "P6" or the 6-part business development recipe. Here it is:

Your First Business Development Recipe: P6

1. PACKAGE a clear and compelling offer
2. PRESENT this offer again and again
3. To different groups of targeted PEOPLE
4. That PERCEIVE they need what you are offering
5. Who PREFER you over your competitors?
6. And they can PAY for what they buy from you.

Now if you are thinking that this recipe sounds simplistic, you should know that just because something sounds easy does not really mean that it is easy to achieve. To illustrate the P6 Recipe I'll now turn it over to Jason Ciment. Much of this can be found in his book, *I need More Clients*, and is geared to people who provide services for their customers. I believe it is easily applicable to businesses that provide products also.

Take it away, Jason.

Package & Present: What People Miss

Let's start with the first two ingredients:
- Packaging your offer, and
- Presenting it in front of more and more people again and again.

What these ingredients suggest is more subtle than you think because people tend to read them at face value and miss out on the nuances.

For ongoing success in a transactional business, you need to know there is a market ready to both buy what you are selling and pay the price you are asking. Whether the market exists or you create it, you need ready and willing buyers – whether it's a product or a service.

Let's start with the offer. Whether it's a service or a product, your offer should ideally follow a pattern where it is:

- Defined
- Refined
- Precise, and
- Compelling

THE MILLIONAIRE PRISONER: PART 3

Ask 2 questions. What problem are you solving? For whom are your solving it? Use a telescope to look at the end result and then work backwards to develop your communication and engagement strategy.

You can "sex up" your messaging with "neuro-linguistic programming" (e.g. mind tricks that sort of hypnotize the reader to take certain actions) and savvy marketing copy, but plainly and simply, there has to be a point where the mechanics of your value propositions must be conveyed to visitors so that "they understand what you are offering" clearly and quickly.

Know How To Package Your "Offer"

In a certain sense, you want to first design the whole tapestry of what you can do and then thread the need throughout your design to take care of the details.

The precursor to "packaging your offer" is to first know as much as you can about what is being offered in the marketplace of competitors.

If you want to frame your service offerings in such a way that you look appealing and stand out from other providers of similar services, you need to dig much deeper than you might expect to really understand what it is you can do for clients that makes you seem more desirable than other providers.

The act of "packaging your offer" is merely a way of saying you need to be more expressive and find a way to break through the white noise so you can gain attention to your (hopefully) unique brand.

What you want to convey with your brand is the expectation of EXCELLENCE – which is not just about the output on your website. It's also about the input. What are you doing to be excellent? What are you reading? What are you eating? What are you doing to produce a celebration of excellence that finds its way into your core values?

To start with, the "packaging" ecosystem also describes the process of highlighting your offer in a way that commands attention of the viewer. Let's try this analogy by borrowing some marketing techniques from the automobile industry.

Just because cars get you from here to there, does not mean all cars are equal. Nor does it mean that people perceive cars the same.

Two effective ways manufacturers distinguish their cars by:

- Designing cars with varied features and different price tags
- Building showrooms and promotional campaigns that set their cars apart from each other (and competitor's cars).

In the context of a prison pen pal website, we can take the analogy of a car manufacturer and learn some valuable lessons. Each of the pen pal process is like a feature of a car.

Just like two cars can have 4-cylinder engines that perform differently, you can have two websites both doing pen pals that provide different levels of service – even within the same or similar areas of pen pals. But this distinction in terms of features is only part of the decision-making process for a consumer who buys a car or a person looking to find a pen pal.

Don't Forget The "Selling" Mindset

THE MILLIONAIRE PRISONER: PART 3

Remember, the automotive customer needs to be "sold" before committing to make a purchase. Just because a car has certain features does not mean a purchase is forthcoming. And this is where "packaging the offer" of the P6 Recipe can add value to our analysis.

In the same way a car company like Toyota builds a website and drives traffic to the website (and to its physical showrooms) by running commercials on TV, print ads in newspapers, streaming video ads online and broadcast spots on radio, a law firm often has to undergo a similar step-by-step marketing process.

Toyota needs to get its cars in front of buyers again and again because cars are not usually an impulse buy. Toyota has to run TV ads repeatedly, build beautiful show rooms usually in highly trafficked areas, create glossy magazine displays and showcase the features of its cars online in beautiful videos merely to package the value of its cars in a way that commands attention in a busy arena.

A business needs to do the same thing by starting with building a website and in some cases the corollary social media properties such as Facebook, Twitter, and LinkedIn. And that is just the essence of the "packaging" framework.

What People Misunderstand About "Packaging" An Offer

1. People think "packaging" is just saying what YOU do instead of saying what you do for YOUR CLIENTS that produces results.
2. Prospects in a service business need to be sold again and again.

3. Packaging leads ultimately to trusting – which is something you have to earn because it's not given freely by your clients.

4. A "me too" brochure website can never compete with a "professionally intentioned" website.

Packaging is a mindset you need to embrace that says "I am going to find a way to talk to the clients I want to reach in a way THEY want to be talked to so I can get under their radar and establish a hypnotic connection that starts the process of connecting each of them into a prospect and ultimately into a lead."

Since my primary area of expertise is about growing your client funnel through online methods, your internet presence must also package your service offerings in such a way that you look like you can not only deliver the "goods" but also outperform your competitors.

This goal does not mean that your website has to be expensive and have the latest gadgets and apps. But your website has to be presentable and that's what we are going to talk about with the 2nd ingredient of P6.

"Presenting" Is Being Sensitive To The Bounce Movement

Your website needs to be CLEAN AND INTUITIVE so that people will quickly know what you do and like what they see before they either worry about figuring out how good you are or worse, leave the site.

I think of this moment of encounter as a test of whether that visitor will decide to stay or leave (i.e., bounce). That decision moment happens fast – so fast, the person does not even realize a decision is being made.

THE MILLIONAIRE PRISONER: PART 3

(WIIFM) What's In It For Me?

Will your visitor stay, or bounce? The Bounce Movement occurs in the lizard part of your brain – the instinctive part of your brain that has existed and has been evolving since the creation of man. This part of your brain NEEDS to know "what this page is offering to do for me" – what marketers call the "what's in it for me" syndrome.

Winning The 6 Second War

When we create a commercial website for a client, one of our initial discussions concerns what we want to happen at that moment of encounter when a person first lands on any page of the website we've built. We think we have less than 6 seconds.

First-time visitors don't need to know if your web page is good or bad at this point. They just need to know what the offer is that they see – and on some primal level "if it is safe to even be on this page."

There is a lot of crossovers between packaging and presenting an offer because once you have figured out what your clients want to hear (in regard to what services you offer), you have to find ways to get this message across in ways that it will be received. And because of the "engagement moment" concept, you've got just a few seconds to sustain a connection with visitors to your website.

Beware of the TMI Pitfalls

Just be careful not to distract visitors with too much info at this initial stage. Even trying to convey the message that you have been doing this for 25 years could sometimes be TMI (too many ingredients).
What most people misunderstand about presenting online.

    1. Timing is critical. You can't throw a plate of spaghetti at someone and expect them to find one noodle that meets their needs. Your messaging needs to come in stages so that you can coax people step by step through your brand value ecosystem.
    2. It's not necessarily what you say, but how you say it that matters even more.
    3. This is why images and videos are so powerful because they can transform any message into something more "presentable."

Think of your website as very shiny container that has to attract and keep someone's attention in such a way that your value propositions (i.e. your services) can be conveyed before someone leaves the site.
    Who are these people we have to target with our offers?
    We can more formally address audience targeting by revisiting our P6 recipe and looking at the third ingredient which is People.

Avoid mass exposure. Get in front of the "Right People"

This is a great segue into something my SEO (search engine optimization) team internally describes as AUDIENCE SEGMENTATION. This is the process of looking at your total audience of potential customers and clients and breaking this audience up into multiple smaller like-minded audiences. There is a strict logic to this mindset.

Your business can't be <u>everything to everyone</u>.
But your business can be <u>everything to someone</u>.

The more you can find people who think you are "their everything", the more business you should be able to bring in – again and again.

Let's put this into concrete terms with an example in a totally different industry so that we don't get overwhelmed with automotive examples.

A vegan restaurant (let's use "Real Food Daily" (RFD) since it's near where I live in Los Angeles) has a greater chance to increase its revenue base if they can consistently appeal individually to each of the four different types of patrons one generally finds in a vegan restaurant.

A vegan restaurant often has various types of customers:

1. People who are lactose intolerant.
2. People who avoid animal products.
3. People who eat it periodically (healthier lifestyle).
4. People who love eating fake meat with fake cheese on fake bread – nothing wrong with that of course.

And it's a viciously successful cycle because the more that patrons feel that the restaurant is catering to their needs, the more successful RFD will be in attracting these customers time and time again.

Wouldn't this type of audience targeting approach producing more positive outcome for your business if you could reach multiple groups of like-minded clients?

RFD has to get into the mindset of these multiple segments of patrons. And then has to come up with a strategy to get its brand in front of these groups of customers to drive them into the restaurant. Since I'm really focused on marketing a business online, let's talk about what RFD should be doing with its www.Realffood.com website.

Clearly it needs to reach out to more customers online and get its menu in front of them – and if not the menu, at least the name of the restaurant in its location and the fact that it is a Vegan (non-dairy, non-meat), food eatery.

People Are Not Just People

RFD needs to connect intimately to each customer base with a messaging strategy that is appealing to that group's needs and tastes.

One of the key approaches to reaching each group is to do some research to find out where each of these groups of potential patrons aggregate and gather online – not necessarily because they are looking for a vegan restaurant – but simply to see if there are places online that RFD can promote itself and be noticed by them.

It Might Be Time to Do a Spock Mind Meld

Consider that identifying and reaching out to your different audience segments may involve two sides of the same coin.

- Get into the minds of your different clients to figure out how to categorize these disparate groups of people into multiple audience segments that share something in common.
- Then you have to analyze each of the audience segments and figure out their browsing habits to see where they go online to find companies like yours and then get in front of them.

Once you have figured out these 2 things, you simply have to initiate <u>moments of introduction</u> which will enable you to…

- Drive these segments of targeted people to your website,
- Introduce them to your brand identity, and
- Pitch them (showcase your offers and your intrinsic value).

By now maybe it's clearer that getting your offer in front of people incorporates many integrated core goals.

1. Know your offer and make it clear to your leads/customers.
2. Wrap the value up in something we call "packaging your offer".
3. Figure out the groups (e.g. segments) of customers to reach.
4. Find out where these customers can be reached online.
5. Find an economic way to get in front of them again and again.

Action Item for You:

Write down things you do for clients; and the types of services you offer.
- Try to categorize your services so it's not just a big laundry list.
- Write down some positioning statements that are like soundbites that describe what you do.
- Write short versions and long versions.

Now put this aside as we continue.

Let's discuss the 4th ingredient of our P6 success recipe – namely, how customers perceive your offer in terms of their own needs.

Catering to Audience "Perceptions"

How your clients think of your services as part of their decision-making process when they hire you or not. What's important to think about is what could be lurking in your customers minds during this decision-making process. And then strive to become the industry expert and be perceived as a market leader.

More Can Be Better With Your Content

The more granular you can be in your web copy (through blog postings for example) about your industry experience, the more chances you will have to both drive more leads (from search rankings) and close those leads due to your perceived industry authority. This of course assumes you have a good website too.

I want to spend a little more time on tactics you can execute on your website and how these items can impact what we should think of going forward as your digital brand identity.

Note that we have to take things a level deeper here. This is because for every business owner who does this, there will be 10 other savvy business owners who also have good domain names and good web copy – and may have read this book (or others like it).

So, the question is: "how do you get a leg up for your service business when there is serious competition in your space for marketing your type of firm online?"

Here are two subtle things you can do that will give you a better chance of connecting your professional services to the people and companies that need them or will make referrals to someone else.
1. Give some of your individual services a brand name.

2. Get a vanity phone number that makes an impact.

The idea behind a brand name is to give people the impression of two things: (1) that this is not your first time to the dance; and (2) that you have created a process around your service.

Let me explain this further.

People naturally are attracted to systems that suggest success. They don't want to be Guinea pigs. They want to know that you have a plan which you have done before and that you can repeat again for them – even if it has to be customized and personalized for their situation.

Divers have a system they call "plan the dive, dive the plan" which reinforces itself every time they dive.

Airplane pilots have a very cumbersome checklist because one item missed can mean a plane crash.

How to put these two subtle ideas into practice:

Take an ordinary handbook you have used for years. Start calling it "The Bulletproof Prisoner Handbook." All of a sudden, the boring handbook has become bulletproof and it's focused on prisoners. When a prisoner sees a business offering a bulletproof handbook, don't you think that is going to make a huge impression and shock them out of their trance of wanting to ignore the information about your handbook, just like they ignore everyone else's handbook description too?

Like the weightlifter hitting the 16th repetition, or the guys from Spinal Tap hitting 11 on the volume dial, you can turn it up a notch with the branding strategy above.

Put a Trademark symbol ™ after the handbook name to give it that official stamp that says you didn't just name your process (that helps prisoners), you protected your process, too. If you want, you can even make an acronym out of the name of the handbook. (B.P.H. for my example above). All these little subtleties are building blocks to be used in the game of connecting more intimately with your target audiences.

Are You Geared for Referrals?

Let's review where we are before we get to the 5th ingredient of our P6 success formula.

1. Your firm offers services.
2. Your firm specializes in these services.
3. You have done an audience segmentation analysis and learned that there are specific industries to target in your geographic reach that have a big demand for your services.
4. You have created landing pages on your website for each of these audience segments describing some of the services you can offer that are contextualized to each reader.
5. You have created specialized content in the form of blogs, articles and/or videos to address each audience segment.

Be Preferred & Win The "Would You Rather" Game

The 5th ingredient says: "Do things that inspire trust" so that you can convince people to PREFER you over alternative choices.

When people reach a web page there is a 3-fold challenge that exists in order to win their trust and keep them from leaving. In the visitor's mind, there are 3 roadblocks (like a toll-gate) with security guards who are instructed to tell the visitor to leave the site unless 3 needs are satisfied:

1. The site is clear about what it is about.
2. The site is clear about who is being addressed.
3. The site is clear about why it should be trusted.

If you have a web page and you want your digital branding message to grab your visitor's attention and bypass the mental (and distrustful) security guards, you must address the following items.

Your Website Needs To Inspire Trust

There are many ways to INSPIRE TRUST and most of them are pretty much under the radar but become quite visible in a negative if you don't adhere to these rules. Here are just a few examples of things a business can do on its website to inspire trust:

- Avoid typos on the website.
- Make sure all the links work (do 404 testing monthly).
- Showcase industry awards.
- Highlight years of experience in specific industries.
- Signup for at least one social media account like Facebook, Twitter or LinkedIn and put the links on your website.
- Match the visual imagery and branding of your website inside your social media pages.
- Your Facebook page should appear visually related to your website.
- If you have partners, then have Rich Team Profiles with good photos and strong web copy (that is more than just a few boring sentences or "me too" paragraphs).
- Publish to a blog at least 2x per month to show that you are current with relevant trends.
- If the blog is just for fun, that can be a powerful "trust" strategy building rapport in a non-business way.

- Have a fresh, compelling looking website that is not more than two years out of date in terms of styling.
- Promote a YouTube video which presents something more compelling than just text and images on a web page.
- Display testimonials and references from clients or other authorities that would matter to each audience segment.
- Write case studies (and drop names) that people will recognize.
- Don't use photos from image libraries that are inappropriate.
- Make it easy and intuitive to navigate the website.
- Display contact info very clearly on every page.
- If physical location matters, display the address on all pages.
- To get people to trust that you can deliver the goods [or services], you have to invest in goodwill and create an online identity that supports your brand.
- Present website visitors with an engaging story.
- Present your firm as competent, timely, and endorsed.
- Add likeability factors that tell visitors that you are both really good at what you do and that people agree with this and like working with you.
- Don't be a jerk – unless being a jerk is something you think people want.
- Be cool. Be fun. Be desirable. Be easy.

Connect Intimately With Your Messaging

People love good listeners, right? When you are listening to someone, you are validating that person's feelings.

Wouldn't you agree that if you could make people feel that your website is a "good listener," they would respond more positively to your offer because you seem more credible and likeable? Before you can even think about what to write about and what keywords you need, you have to think about the mindset of your clients (current, prospective and future).

Customize Your Solutions to Address Specific Pain Points

Here are the components I believe you should include in a high-performance communication strategy that will succeed at transforming prospective leads into existing clients.

1. What are the individual PAIN POINTS you can identify for each audience segment?
2. The more details you can uncover, the stronger you can make your landing pages and overall messaging.
3. What solutions can you provide that address the pain points?
4. Again, it's the same principles. The more details you can provide that individualize your approach for each audience, the more you will keep people interested in your website.
5. What about your background suggests that you are any good at producing a positive outcome?
6. Just because you are able to do something does not easily translate into you doing that thing competently – let alone with excellence.
7. Just because you might be good – think testimonials, years of experience – you still need to communicate that you can:

a) Act timely.
b) Act responsibly.
c) Be fair.

Let's put this all together.
Can you transmit something that suggests you are a good listener? You need to take the time out what the client needs. You need to address these needs on your website content through blog postings, videos, images, testimonials and even surveys.
Just so we are clear, you really have to "Know Your Audience". This means you have to do research to learn about your different audience segments and their habits, needs, goals, and desires. And part of the segmentation is to create demographic and psychographic profiles which you can use in your landing page copy too.

Address Each Audience Segment Individually

As we complete this section on expansive Audience Segmentation Analysis, I will tell you that there are 4 groups you should always look to communicate with:

- Current Clients and Customers
- Prospective Clients and Customers
- Competitors
- Referral Sources (Channel partners and Friends)

Use Intermediaries to Reach More People

This is a good time to talk about a fantastic method of getting in front of people over and over again. It is when you can work through facilitators that can make introductions that connect you with clients. I always encourage clients to build more relationships with middle men – intermediaries.

Look for scenarios with other people that can make digital introductions that connect you with potential clients. That wondrous moment of introduction can be artificially induced and occur with the help of an electronic intermediary:

- A search engine ranking
- A PPC ad
- A website mention (with a link to your site)
- A YouTube video (with a link to your site)
- A blog posting (with a link to your site)

Are You Still Holding Your Engagement Ring?

Let's uncover the last and most important P in our recipe – PAYMENT.

Getting in front of those targeted groups of people that can actually <u>PAY for what you are offering</u>. Think of it this way. It's nice to go to the dance, but not if you leave the party without a date. It's great to date seriously, but greater to marry. Business school books are filled with stories of companies with great ideas that people said they wanted but weren't ready to pay for.

Sometimes your product might be ready before its time and the "need" is not there yet. You can't force it either. Other times the cost is simply too much of a barrier to entry to enable your company to "take off" and be successful. As much as we've been discussing "Audience segmentation"

and "offer differentiation", you have to qualify your customers.
   Even obvious things need to be stated and restated once in a while.
   1. Ask tough questions up front. Don't waste resources on people that are not likely to be good clients (or good lead sources).
   2. Use the contact form on your website to give people choices where they can almost self-select themselves out of your orbit.
   3. If an online form includes an option that says "choose a service", if the list does not include the service they want, they will abandon the form.
   4. If you put a price range down starting at $5,000 for example, and if they have a $2,000 budget, they won't bother you.
   5. Of course, this also has risk because a $2,000 client can often be upsold into the $5,000 level. And there is a similar risk by listing a limited range of services. People may feel you don't offer the service they think they need.

Time for a Homework Assignment
Pull out the notebook with your list of services (i.e., offers) from earlier.

- Make a list of 3 competitor websites and visit their sites.
- Write down the services they are offering.
- Write down the types of clients they are targeting.
- List keyword phrases and topics, they are using that people would be typing into Google as a relevant search query.

- Print out pages from these sites that grab your interest.
- Mark up the areas of the web pages that inspire trust.

(Refer to the list of trust factors mentioned previously).

- Review a few pages from your own site in light of what you've learned so far. Make notes about changes you might want to address. Don't do them yet because there are more tactics coming that you'll need to consider first.
- Write down your own list of audience segments to see how many niches you can identify that would be good candidates for individualized landing pages.
- Go through your own offers (e.g., practice areas) and break them down into discrete pieces with more detailed explanations.
- Look through your digital media inventory to see if you can find images and photos and videos to inject into your website and social media properties.

It's time for me to leave you now. But this doesn't have to be the end of our conversation. If you want to discover other recipes for getting more clients and customers, I invite you to check out my services at https://www.GetVisible.com.

CHAPTER SIXTEEN

How To Take Your Business To The Money Moon

"I'd rather shoot for the moon and miss than shoot for the gutter and make it."

– Danny Trejo

An Expert Wealth Manager Talks About Taking Your Business To the Money Moon!

Justin Krane (www.Jkrance.com) is a Certified Financial Planner™ and money strategist for small business owners. Here he gives you five things to help you take your business to the moon:

"To the Moon Baby. It's time to seriously grow your business. I want you to take your business to the moon baby. Seriously. Your time is like... Right. Now.

If I could wave some weird funky magic wand over your biz-ness, shnizz-ness, and turn it into gold – here is what I would want you to have: these 5 things. They are:

1. A great business model
2. Profits of 10% of sales.
3. Cash money in the Bank.

4. Know your numbers.
5. The right message to the right market.

I manage money. But my real passion is creating money strategies for small business owners. I am a money strategy nut. I'm wild cray-cray. So here I go...
   Numero Uno! We can't even get started until you master this one simple concept. Your business model. Yep.

So how do you make money? What is it that you specifically do to get paid? And how easy is it for you to do this? Do you get paid one time, or is it recurring?

I hate to pick on realtors. But they have one of the hardest business models I have seen. They work like 18 hours a day. And if that escrow doesn't close – they don't get paid. If someone doesn't qualify for a loan, realtors don't get paid. If a buyer has cold feet, the realtor doesn't get paid. I could go on and on. You get the point.

Also...can you scale your business? Get any leverage doing it? Scale and leverage is about getting more with less. Here are examples:

1. Instead of working with one client at a time, you could work with 4 clients at a time – in a group environment.
2. Investing in some software for $100, which allows you to be more productive and do an additional $500 in sales.

Action Plan!

THE MILLIONAIRE PRISONER: PART 3

Answer those questions up above in bold. Write down your answers right here in the margin. You got this! Bottom line, you need a business model that allows you to grow, and make profits.

Speaking of profits, that is <u>Numero Dos!</u> Here's the deal. You can have sales. <u>But you need profits!</u>

I want your profits to be at least 10% of your sales. Or more! Example – Sales of $5000. That means after all expenses, including what you pay yourself – <u>even what you pull out of the business to live</u> – you need to have a profit of 10%, or $500.

If your business can't make money, you won't make money. You will run out of money. You also need to have a profit mindset. That means you need to be thinking about your sales – and if you will have enough sales to pay your business expenses.

It's about charging what you are worth. It's about not throwing money away. Really challenging yourself to make money.

You are running an empire. Be a prosperity thinker. You can create the financial life that you want for yourself. But you need to take action. Don't forget about that profit mindset. <u>10% or more as you go to the moon!</u>

Action Plan!

What are your average sales? Multiply that number by 10%. That is what your biz needs to make at a minimum. Write that number in the margin right here.

<u>Numero Tres!</u> Cash. Cash money.

Your business needs to keep some cash lying around. If you have a fat stack of cash – you can say no to people. Saying no is huge. The worst thing is when you take on projects and clients just for the money. Because you need the money.

So here is what I want you to do. I want you to have an emergency fund for your business account. Make a list of what your fixed monthly expenses are. Keep 1-2 months of those fixed expenses in the bank. Just leave it there. It's your little security blanket.

Action Plan!

Having this amount of money in the bank will let you sleep at night. So, what are your average monthly expenses? Write it in the margin of this book. Keep that amount of money in cash.

<u>Numero Quattro!</u> How do you even spell 4 in Spanish!?!

You need to be tracking you numbers.

But here's the deal. You don't have to do this by yourself. Just hire someone. A bookkeeper. An assistant. Anyone who can help you with the numbers.

Every business needs to have a set of books. But it is really about which numbers make a difference in your business. Start with the ones we have discussed: cash and profits. Just those 2. Have your helper person just email you these 2 numbers every 1-2 weeks. Literally – just an email. Knowledge is power baby. The more you know – the better decisions you will be able to make.

I got one nugget for you on tracking. This is about your sales. But I want to use this "losing weight analogy." You can get on the scale every day to see what you weigh. Or you can track the activities that will drive how much weight you could lose.

You could track your calories. You could track how many days a week you exercise. So why not track the stuff that will drive your sales in business? So, what are the things in your business that will drive sales?

Sales conversations? The size of your email list? How many people visit your site? How much hair gel you use? Are you still reading this!!!? LOL!

So here is your 3 part

Action Plan!

- Write down the person who will track your numbers for you.
- Write down 2 numbers you will track.
- Write down 2 things that you will track that will drive your sales.

Numero Cinco!

I love money strategy. Can you tell? But if you can dial this one thing in, and get it going real good, your biz could go to the moon...

Here I go...

You need the right message hitting the right pain point hitting the right target market.

You think that's easy? Boy. Lemme tell ya. It is a major work in progress for me. Where does the money stuff come in on this one? You are going to have to hire people to help you get this nailed down. Marketing experts, surveys, analysis, etc.

Keep this in the back of your mind as you build your business. See you at the moon!

The Millionaire Prisoner's Resource Guide

The best book I have ever read about tracking numbers, including numbers you've never heard of is:

- *No B.S. Ruthless Management of People and Profit* by Dan S. Kennedy (www.NoBSBooks.com)

> "I'd rather shoot for the moon and miss than shoot for the gutter and make it." – Danny Trejo

CHAPTER SEVENTEEN

The Power of Backlinks

"It's the little details that are vital. Little things make big things happen."

– John Wooden

Here's a little trick that can improve your search engine rankings for keyword phrases found on these niche pages. When you write the individualized content for each "niche audience" page on your website, add some links to OTHER websites that are authoritative for that niche.

So, if you are writing about prison pen pals in Illinois, link to the Illinois Department of Corrections site, the Illinois Prison Talk Online Page, and an Illinois prison blog site.

When Google sees you Linking Out to other websites – rather than just having links coming INTO your website – that shows in a counter-intuitive way that you are more of a resource, which Google loves.

That's what you can do on your website to climb up the search rankings. But how do you climb up the rankings even more? By getting other websites to link back to your site.

The Power of Backlinks

Most of this section was, and is, taught by online business strategist Jason Cimet (www.GetVisible.com) in his book, *I*

Need More Clients. I have reproduced it here with his written permission.

Where do backlinks come from? A backlink simply refers to a link that appears on another website that links to your website. How do you get a backlink? There are many ways to get a backlink. Here are some examples:

1. Someone is asked for free to link to your website.

2. The site owner is paid (whether money or some other exchange of value) to link to your website. This is called "black hat."

3. You build a different website and link that one to your first website. (This could be considered "grey hat.")

4. You submit a form online that posts the information (including a link to your website) on someone else's website.

5. The site owner discovers your webpage and volunteers to link to it (this is what Google wants to see happen naturally).

There are hundreds of techniques to get quality backlinks. The above examples are just a framework you can reference that describes many different variations of how to acquire backlinks to a website.

Here's the core rule in regards to back links and rankings. <u>The more links you get on websites that are contextually relevant to your website AND that are themselves considering to be AUTHORITATIVE</u> (read this to

THE MILLIONAIRE PRISON: PART 3

mean powerful) by Google's measurements, the higher your rankings will climb.

The process of building backlinks is also referred to as OFF PAGE optimization. Websites that want to increase their organic rankings in a competitive marketplace must grow the backlinks to their sites.

Backlinks Are Not Democratic

It's important to understand that this urgency to grow links is not like a traditional election where you need to accumulate as many votes as you can get by a certain point in time.

First of all, you have to keep acquiring backlinks pretty much forever. Secondly, votes are not treated equally. The value of each vote is NOT the same. A backlink from a legal blog post on CNN or an article by a lawyer on Huffington Post is simply far more powerful to a law firm than a link on a health and wellness site from a guy in his garage who has little traffic or engagement with his content.

SEO companies are constantly on the prowl to find ways to acquire links for their clients that look natural and don't cost too much to acquire. Of course, this idea of costing too much is a relative concept because if you spend $5,000 on efforts to get an article published on a site like CNN with a backlink, it could very well be worth that sum.

You may be wondering how a backlink can have a cost associated with it if Google's guidelines strictly point out that should not pay websites for backlinks.

Let's use a prisoner rights attorney in Illinois to illustrate an answer. Our client has written a blog post on a trend in the prison scene in Illinois where correctional officers are accused of stealing prisoners' property because they are paid low wages (OK, it's a wacky example but it caught your attention).

We need to reach out to other websites that have content that is relevant to this topic and let these sites now about our client's new article. And, our goal is to get these sites to post something about the article and link to the article from their website.

There are two intertwined goals here.

- First, is to get contextually relevant sites to link to the article.
- Second, is to get powerful sites (that may not be very contextually related) to put a backlink on their site to my client's site. This process is called acquiring "link juice."

So where does this idea come from that there is a cost to a backlink? Simply, it's a labor cost to identify and to then reach out to these sites. Many companies simply can't afford to execute these types of outreach services. Public relations firms are so expensive because the bulk of their work involves finding and connecting with people that can publish.

The Pursuit of Backlinks as A Virtual Partnership

If you do research on backlink tactics, you will see that there are all sorts of ways you can get backlinks from other sites. Some kosher, some not so kosher. Some free and some not so free.

THE MILLIONAIRE PRISON: PART 3

I want to talk about PARTNERING with other sites not from an actual "reach out and contact them standpoint," but rather from a "mindset" standpoint where the backlinks will flow naturally because of the content you are guided to create in this partnering mindset process.

If we all agree that rankings (in a competitive environment) are impacted by quantity and quality of your backlinks (i.e., LINK JUICE), then it also means we can agree that if you give someone a good reason to link to your website it might be easier to get the link. If you start thinking about what you could do as a GOOD PARTNER for these other websites to provide THEM what value, you may start finding them more willing to link to you – thus, an easier pathway to backlinks.

Let me give you an example.

Acquiring Backlinks Starts With In-Depth Research:

Instead of thinking first about the topic you want to write about because you see something trending in BuzzFeed, look instead for powerful sites that would be great to get backlinks from and see what kind of content they are publishing and promoting.

As you evaluate the themes within their website content and the audiences they are engaging, consider what type of content you could create for them that would induce the Pavlovian response you need – a request by them to link to your site.

If you view yourself as a joint venture partner to other websites, you will likely create keyword rich content you already need but have it geared for distribution on other sites simply because your content will be more resonant to their needs.

Here's a super-fragilistic type of secret way to find the topics you can write about that will get shared more often. It's so simple that it has a brand name associated with it: "skyscraper content". For more on that you can look up the term on Google from Brian Dean to see more about this technique. I will present a variation of it here.

Content Should Stick Out Like A Skyscraper And Be Noticed

Find an article that has been shared a lot online in that has a lot of views. Obviously, you want to look for a topic that is relevant to your business or target market. Put together your own version of that article. I don't mean copy it. I mean write something on the same topic but with your own perspective.

One of these statistically proven in best pieces of content you can write for this purpose is a top 10 list. You don't need to stick to 10. You can use "Seven ways to…" or something like that. (See *"Seven Ways A Prisoner Could Make Money From Artwork"* in this book.) Just make a top something list and that will be usually more popular than a non-list type of content piece. You can also create the same content in the form of a video or image slideshow and then load it up on YouTube or Slideshare.

You can even find someone else's top 10 list and write your own top 15 list incorporating the ideas from the top 10 list. Just give appropriate attributions and put a spin on the top 15 list with your personal flavor.

Before you actually publish the article or top ten posting on your site, you need to put the Tees in place. You need to reach out to at least 5 or 10 of the websites (and their owners) that shared the original article you found. Connect with them and let them know you are putting out something that might resonate with their readers. This technique is a great – though – labor intensive way to build your backlink arsenal.

One other type of content you could create is an "infographic" which is a visually better way of writing about statistical data. For more, see *Infographics: The Power of Visual Storytelling* by Jason Lankow, Josh Ritehie, and Ross Crooks.

A Prisoner Example of Using Backlinks

Now that you understand all that, you may be thinking that it doesn't apply to you because you're in prison. Or that you can't take advantage of it because you don't have a website or a blog. If you want to get pen pals (most of us would like to get mail) you can use a version of this to backlink to your pen pal profile or Facebook profile page. Here's what I mean.

In *Pretty Girls Love Bad Boys,* prisoner King Guru talks about posting online so you can send girls you meet to those sites to see your stuff. That's great (and so is his book), but I want you to think about utilizing the content you post on these sites as a lead magnet for pen pals (or whatever you're trying to attract). Right now, I have a pen pal profile on WriteAPrisoner.com. I could write an article and post it on the websites that post prisoners' writing for free and then at the end of the article say something like this:

"Did you like what you read? Would you like to get to know me more? I can be reached by clicking on the below link: https://writeaprisoner.com/inmates/joshua-kruger-k-50216"

You don't want to say, "check me out on WriteAPrisoner" without your link. That would give them too many options besides you. The goal is to provide them one clicks through to your profile. Once you set up a Facebook page or your own website, then you should direct the links to your pages there. Keep writing and posting original content and you never know what will happen. I once posted a short blog about an all-white cat that was sitting in the sun on a Boulder next to the exercise yard at my prison. A girl I knew from back in the days saw and wrote me. That led to visits, phone conversations, and money in my trust fund account. The key is to "get visible" by posting online. Here are some places that will post your writing online for free:

APWA
198 College Hill Road
Clinton, NY 13323-1218

Journal of Prisoners on Prisons
c/o Justin Piche, PhD
Department of Criminology
University of Ottawa
Ottawa, Ontario
K1N 6N5
Canada

The Marshall Project
156 West 56th St., Suite 701
New York, NY 10010

Minutes Before Six

THE MILLIONAIRE PRISON: PART 3

2784 Homestead Road #301
Santa Clara, CA 95051

Prisons Foundation
2512 Virginia Ave., NW
#58043
Washington, DC 20037

Prison Society
230 S. Broad St., Ste #605
Philadelphia, PA 19102

Walk In Those Shoes
c/o Kimberly Carter
POB 70092
Henrico, VA 23255

Do not send the same essay to each of these places. Try to write different nonfiction articles for each of these places above. Send SASE's to get their submission guidelines first so you know what rules to follow before you send in your articles.

Recommended Resource

For more about the power of backlinks and a way more in-depth look at all things web-based, get a copy of:

- *Ultimate Guide to Link Building* by Eric Ward and Garrett French

You can also listen to an audio book on the GTL Tablet about link building at:

• Backlinks – *Increasing Website Traffic And Page Ranking With Backlinking*

CHAPTER EIGHTEEN

3 Mistakes Prisoner-Service businesses Make and How to Correct Them!

"If you don't have a clear competitive advantage, develop one."

– Peter Drucker

Most Prisoner-Service Businesses Are Owned By Lazy, Incompetent, and Stupid People!!

I'm sure the above headline just got some people's attention. And I'm sure it made some people mad also? I don't care. Because it's the truth. It's how I feel. It's how most prisoners feel. These businesses don't know how to serve a captive audience. (Pun intended!) Let me tell you a few mistakes they make. Then I'll tell you how it should work for a business that wants to create lifetime customer value from a prisoner. If you have a business that does anything for prisoners you need to pay attention.

A business normally places a small classified ad in *Prison Legal News* (or some other magazine that prisoners read), and asks the prisoner to send in a SASE (Self-addressed stamped-envelope) for more information. Nothing wrong with that. So, the prisoner does as told. In return, the company sends their sales brochure and literature. Here are three mistakes I see when we get the sales pieces:

1. They have blank pages in them. Why waste a perfect time and place to explain who you are in why you're the best company to serve me – the prisoner? Because they are lazy and don't want to take the time to write it up. Or they are too stupid to even know why they can help us? Either way, it's a huge mistake. No page should be left blank in these sales pieces.

2. They send ONLY a thin trifold brochure? WTF? I'm guessing they do this because that's what they see everyone else doing? Stupid. The prisoner has sent in his/her SASE. That means you have an envelope with proper first-class postage on it. You can send up to one ounce of weight in that envelope. It's your duty to use all of that one ounce. Not skimp because you're lazy. You can take 5 pieces of typing paper and fold them in half and put them together to make a 20-page booklet or sales flyer! Can they write a 20-page booklet or flyer? If they can't, then hire someone to do it. You can hire me if you want. But most companies can't, or don't, because they're too lazy or incompetent to do it.

3. Lastly, their brochures are filled with the features of the product or service and not the benefits. Huge mistake. Explain to us prisoners what the benefit will be for us if we use your product or service. And if you can, prove it to us by having testimonials of past users telling us what they gained as a result of using it. We should read your sales brochure and believe that we'll miss out if we don't order right away. Most of these businesses don't know how to do this.

THE MILLIONAIRE PRISON: PART 3

Okay, let's say the company has got these first three things right, and I like what they're saying. So, I send in my money and buy their product or service. They get my money and perform their service and I never hear from them again. WOW! They just made a huge mistake. I'm serving life in prison. I'm an author and thought leader for prisoners. I got a little money to spend. For all those reasons the company should be going out of their way to make me feel like I'm their ONLY customer in the world. But most of them don't. Because they don't understand "lifetime customer value." I've been locked up for over 26 years of my life. I have only seen a few companies who got it right. One is Edward R. Hamilton Bookseller company. I've spent probably close to a thousand dollars with them ordering books over the years. Why? Because they send me catalog after catalog. When I'm done with a catalog, I pass it on to another prisoner who may, or may not, order some books. Edward R. Hamilton gets it. Most don't.

I will use a prisoner pen pal company as an example because they are easy to pick on because most of them get it wrong. But here's how it should go if they really wanted to get rich.

First, when a prisoner pays for a service that should not be the end of it. The company should build a relationship with the prisoner. Why? Because most pen pal relationships go stale. The prisoner will need more pen pals in the future. Don't you want your company to be the one they come back to trying to get more pen pals? So, give them a reason to come back to you and your company.

Second, these companies don't offer anything besides posting an ad online. If I just spent $50 to go online for a year,

I might be willing to spend more money if they could "upsell" me on more/better services? None of them do it because they don't have any better services to offer. That's a bad strategy. It would be better to send your customers a simple questionnaire asking them what else would they pay for and how much would they pay? If you get the same responses from different prisoners, then there's your gold mine. Go create the solution to their problem and advertise it to them. Most of these businesses won't do it because they are lazy. So, they don't get rich. Penacon has stepped their game up on this though!

Here's a simple strategy that would go a long way. Every prisoner who has paid for a product or service should get a birthday card from the company wishing them a Happy Birthday! I've seen only two companies do this for me. Freebird publishers and Prison Inmates Online. Why don't other companies do it? It means a lot. It doesn't have to be a fancy card. Just a simple card, or even a postcard will do. It doesn't have to say much. Even: "We at (company name) want to wish you a Happy Birthday! Stay safe and be blessed!", would be fine. Who do you think they will remember when it comes time to buy more products, pay for a service, or refer you to their prisoner friends? You bet it will be the company that sent them a birthday card. For that same reason you should also send "Happy Holiday" cards around Thanksgiving/Christmas time.

Another thing they don't do is cultivate the prison "influencers." Do they even know who they are? Do they know how to find them? Mike Enemigo of The Cell Block is one. He has his own "Directory" for prisoners. He lets prisoners make "comments" about the companies in his directory, and he also makes comments based on his

THE MILLIONAIRE PRISON: PART 3

experiences. Do you know him? Have you sent him your sales literature? Have you sent him a birthday card? I have a copy of his <u>Directory</u> in my hands right now. I'm a prisoner. The most important thing for me is the "comments" on each listing if there are some? Let's say I was a prisoner who bought hotshot photos of sexy girls? I'd look up all the sexy photo sellers and see if there are any "comments" on them? There are lots of them. I'm going to use the company that has the best "comments." That's how a prisoner uses Mike's directory, *The Best Resource Directory for Prisoners*. That's how we use *Inmate Shopper*!

Now, if you have the 2020 edition of Mike Enemigo's *The Best Resource Directory For Prisoners*, and look up these sexy photo sellers you'll see one name come up on several of these sexy photo sellers. Troy Shaw in Indiana. Who is he? I don't know. But if I was in the free world and had a company that sold sexy photos, or did any business for prisoners, I'd go to Indiana's DOC's website and look him up. I'd send him my sales literature and he would get a birthday card and a Happy Holidays card also. (All Department of Corrections have websites that list prisoner addresses and birthdays.) Why would I do this for Troy Shaw? Because he has demonstrated the ability to influence my target market! (Hey Troy, if you get some cards in the mail, you're welcome!) Who are the influencers for your customers? Find them, befriend them, and cultivate them.

Back to the prison pen pal websites. If I was them, I'd poach my competitor's customers. Most prisoners who go on prison pen pal websites will not be completely satisfied with the results they get. We always want more pen pals and more hits. One of my best friends, Skylar, has got 27 pen pal hits off one site. But she wants more! We all do. So why not poach your competitors' websites. Their customers are listed there for all to see. Every time they update their page it means they paid more money to do it. By golly here they are – a prisoner who has money to spend. Isn't that their ideal customer? It should be logical that they would want to find these people? Even if you don't have a pen pal business, I'll tell you where to find prisoners. Online. On these prison pen pal websites. Here's what I'd do.

I'd set up a dummy email account and then go subscribe to every new prisoner's account on WriteAPrisoner.com. When they updated their profile, I'd get a notification of it. That would tell me that this prisoner isn't just a one-time buyer. So as soon as I got that notice I would be putting my sales literature in the mail to them that night. I would have a personal letter in it with the opening line in bold that says: "If you're completely satisfied with your pen pal website results, throw this letter away! If not, then maybe I can help you?" My letter would say, "Dear (his/her name)" and not the very impersonal "Dear prisoner" or "Dear potential customer". Then my sales letter would go on to explain to them why I knew about his/her pain and how my company could solve it for them. Doing that I never have to advertise in *PLN* ever again. I'd only place ads in *PLN* if I wanted a quick influx of inquiries and customers.

Most companies won't do something like that above because they don't know who their ideal customer is? Either because they didn't do any market research, or they haven't asked their existing customers. If you have customers or clients, you should know the following:

- What magazines are newsletters do they read?
- What TV shows do they watch?

THE MILLIONAIRE PRISON: PART 3

- What commissary products do they buy?
- Where do they go to for advice?
- What is their #1 problem besides being locked up?

I know six prisoners personally who have spent $100+ a year on pen pal services at one time or another. (Seven, if you count me in that group.) What do we all have in common? We all read books, subscribe to magazines, watch "Love After Lockup", and want more pen pals. Do you know how to find out this information from your customers? All you have to do is ask them. Especially your best customers – the ones who spend the most. Those are the ones who you should want to clone. You can. If you know who they really are? Because once you do, you'll know where to find them. Then it will be up to you to cultivate them. Use a customer/client questionnaire to find out all about your best customers.

By using birthday cards and customer questionnaires a prisoner-service business could rise to the top. Here are some other ways to do it.

- Use a newsletter mailed monthly to your customers (or weekly if it's by email, like Corrlinks.)
- Start a podcast an get it onto the GTL and JPay tablets. (Or give 15 minute/30 minute talks with tips and strategies that are on the tablet for prisoners to listen to.)
- Hold contests and sweepstakes for your customers where they could win a how-to book or something else helpful/useful.
- Practice great customer service with fast responses to orders and complaints. This is the most important one of all. More prisoners complain about having to wait months for response, than anything else.

I could list a hundred or more things that these businesses could do to set themselves apart from the other prisoner-based companies. But most of them won't follow my advice because they are lazy, incompetent, and stupid. I'm glad that you're reading this. It shows me that you're not lazy, incompetent, or stupid. I'll see you at the top!

CONCLUSION

"The object of life is not to be on the side of the masses, but to escape finding oneself in the ranks of the insane."
— Marcus Aurelius

What do you do now? Hopefully you get to work. That's the key to becoming a Millionaire Prisoner – taking what you learn and applying it into your life. To get royalty checks from a book you have to write the book first. Or have someone else write it and you publish it. To make money off artwork you have to put together the piece first. Or get someone else to do it and you sell it. To make money from stocks you have to purchase them. To capitalize on a winning bet in the sports handicapping market you have to place the bet. To have your own business you have to start it. Notice the common denominator in all these examples – <u>you have to do something</u>. You have to start something. Then you have to finish it. See it through. Even if it doesn't end up like you first thought. Keep going! Nothing happens until you start moving. You can accomplish a lot by taking simple steps each day towards your goals. That's how you create momentum. That's how you become unstoppable. So, take the first step and start.

    I would love to hear from you. I live by the philosophy of "teach one, reach one." And I'm still learning. I'd love to learn from you. Tell me about your journey, success, and any tips, tactics, or strategies you may have? If I use them in future books I'll be sure to give you credit as the author and originator. Take time to fill out the questionnaire at the back of this book and send it in. Mike and I plan to keep creating quality how-to products and we listen to our readers. Our motto is, "For prisoners, by prisoners." Help us work for you. Spread the word about The Cell Block and our books. We are sure you won't be disappointed. Be blessed in all that you do.

ABOUT THE AUTHOR

Josh Kruger is *The Millionaire Prisoner*™. He's a Cellpreneur, author, and leading authority on how prisoners can live productive and happy lives by thinking outside the cell, networking, and breaking down carceral barriers.

He and his work has been seen in *The Commercial News, The News Gazette, Prison Legal News, Kite Magazine, Straight Stuntin, Inmate Shopper, The Best Resource Directory for Prisoners, Conscious County Courier,* among others.

In 1999, Josh was arrested for felony murder, home invasion, and robbery. He refused to turn State's evidence against his co-defendant in return for a 20-year sentence. At the subsequent 2000 bench trial he received a directed verdict of acquittal when the State of Illinois refused to participate over an evidence dispute. Josh was released, but eventually rearrested after the State successfully got the not guilty verdict vacated on appeal. See People V. Kruger, 327 Ill.App.3d 839, 764 N.E.2d 138 (4th Dist. Ill. 2002). At the 2003 jury trial, Josh was convicted based on a theory of accountability and sentenced to life in prison without parole. People V. Kruger, 363 Ill.App.3d 1113, 845 N.E.2d 96 (4th Dist. Ill. 2006).

After reading several of Zig Ziglar's books, Josh reached out to the late, great motivational speaker and began corresponding with Ziglar. He adopted Zig's philosophy that you can have everything you want in life if you just help enough people get what they want.

Tired of depending on friends and family for support, the graduate of Crown Financial Ministries decided to leverage his extensive juvenile and adult prison experience into a freelance writing career. In 2011, Josh launched his micro-publishing empire from his maximum-security prison cell by self-publishing two booklets, *How To Get FREE Pen-Pals* and *How to Win Your Football Pool*. Prison authorities seized his property and threw him in segregation by alleging that he was violating prison rules. Not to be dismayed, Josh kept going and published his first book, *The Millionaire Prisoner*. His goal was to help prisoners turn their prison into a stepping-stone to success.

A fierce defender of prisoner rights, especially those under the First Amendment, Josh has filed numerous successful lawsuits challenging prison conditions and bogus censorship practices. See Kruger V. Boland, etal., 15-CV-1261 (C.O. Ill.); Kruger V. Pfister, etal., 15-CV-1325 (C.D. Ill.); Kruger V. Lashbrook, etal., 18-CV-512 (S.C. Ill.); Kruger V. Baldwin, etal., 19-CV-268 (S.D. Ill.); Kruger V. Baldwin, etal., 19-MR-144 (Sangamon County Circuit Court, Ill.); and Kruger V. Lashbrook, etal., 20-CV-24 (S.D. Ill.). He believes that prisoners should have the same rights extended to them that free-world people have, and that the protection afforded by the constitution does not end at the prison gates. He will fiercely defend his name and *The Millionaire Prisoner* brand.

It took Josh only 30 days to write his second book, *Pen Pal Success*, which is based on his personal experiences form behind the iron veil of prison. After the success of both of his books a lot of prisoners started asking him how he did it. So, he wrote *Cellpreneur: The Millionaire Prisoner's Guidebook*, to

THE MILLIONAIRE PRISON: PART 3

show prisoners how-to legally start a business from their prison cell. He also compiled *Celebrity Female Star Power: The Millionaire Prisoner's Address Book* after his cellmate – JuBoy – showed him how much prisoners love celebrities. His latest project, *Prison Picasso* (a two-part series on how to sell arts and crafts), has just been released.

Josh has vowed to never stop writing or fighting for prisoner rights and prison reform. His mission is to change lives, one prisoner at a time. He can be reached at: freejoshkruger@gmail.com.

MIKE ENEMIGO PRESENTS

THE CELL BLOCK

BOOK SUMMARIES

MIKE ENEMIGO is the new prison/street art sensation who has written and published several books. He is inspired by emotion; hope; pain; dreams and nightmares. He physically lives somewhere in a California prison cell where he works relentlessly creating his next piece. His mind and soul are elsewhere; seeing, studying, learning, and drawing inspiration to tear down suppressive walls and inspire the culture by pushing artistic boundaries.

THE CELL BLOCK is an independent multimedia company with the objective of accurately conveying the prison/street experience with the credibility and honesty that only one who has lived it can deliver, through literature and other arts, and to entertain and enlighten while doing so. Everything published by The Cell Block has been created by a prisoner, while in a prison cell.

THE BEST RESOURCE DIRECTORY FOR PRISONERS, $17.95 & $5.00 S/H: This book has over 1,450 resources for prisoners! Includes: Pen-Pal

THE MILLIONAIRE PRISON: PART 3

Companies! Non-Nude Photo Sellers! Free Books and Other Publications! Legal Assistance! Prisoner Advocates! Prisoner Assistants! Correspondence Education! Money-Making Opportunities! Resources for Prison Writers, Poets, Artists! And much, much more! Anything you can think of doing from your prison cell, this book contains the resources to do it!

A GUIDE TO RELAPSE PREVENTION FOR PRISONERS, $15.00 & $5.00 S//H: This book provides the information and guidance that can make a real difference in the preparation of a comprehensive relapse prevention plan. Discover how to meet the parole board's expectation using these proven and practical principles. Included is a blank template and sample relapse prevention plan to assist in your preparation.

CONSPIRACY THEORY, $12.00 & $4.00 S/H: Kokain is an upcoming rapper trying to make a name for himself in the Sacramento, CA underground scene, and Nicki is his girlfriend. One night, in October, Nicki's brother, along with her brother's best friend, go to rob a house of its $100,000 marijuana crop. It goes wrong; shots are fired and a man is killed. Later, as investigators begin closing in on Nicki's brother and his friend, they, along with the help of a few others, create a way to make Kokain take the fall .... The conspiracy begins.

THEE ENEMY OF THE STATE (SPECIAL EDITION), $9.99 & $4.00 S/H: Experience the inspirational journey of a kid who was introduced to the art of rapping in 1993, struggled between his dream of becoming a professional rapper and the reality of the streets, and was finally offered a recording deal in 1999, only to be arrested minutes later and eventually sentenced to life in prison for murder... However, despite his harsh reality, he dedicated himself to hip-hop once again, and with resilience and determination, he sets out to prove he may just be one of the dopest rhyme writers/spitters ever .... At this point, it becomes deeper than rap .... Welcome to a preview of the greatest story you never heard.

LOST ANGELS: $15.00 & $5.00: David Rodrigo was a child who belonged to no world; rejected for his mixed heritage by most of his family and raised by an outcast uncle in the mean streets of East L.A. Chance cast him into a far darker and more devious pit of intrigue that stretched from the barest gutters to the halls of power in the great city. Now, to survive the clash of lethal forces arrayed about him, and to protect those he loves, he has only two allies; his quick wits, and the flashing blade that earned young David the street name, Viper.

LOYALTY AND BETRAYAL DELUXE EDITION, $19.99 & $7.00 S/H: Chunky was an associate of and soldier for the notorious Mexican Mafia -- La Eme. That is, of course, until he was betrayed by those, he was most loyal to. Then he vowed to become their worst enemy. And though they've attempted to kill him numerous times, he still to this day is running around making a mockery of their organization .... This is the story of how it all began.

MONEY IZ THE MOTIVE: SPECIAL 2-IN-1 EDITION, $19.99 & $7.00 S/H: Like most kids growing up in the hood, Kano has a dream of going from rags to riches. But when his plan to get fast money by

THE MILLIONAIRE PRISON: PART 3

robbing the local "mom and pop" shop goes wrong, he quickly finds himself sentenced to serious prison time. Follow Kano as he is schooled to the ways of the game by some of the most respected OGs whoever did it; then is set free and given the resources to put his schooling into action and build the ultimate hood empire...

DEVILS & DEMONS: PART 1, $15.00 & $5.00 S/H: When Talton leaves the West Coast to set up shop in Florida he meets the female version of himself: A drug dealing murderess with psychological issues. A whirlwind of sex, money and murder inevitably ensues and Talton finds himself on the run from the law with nowhere to turn to. When his team from home finds out he's in trouble, they get on a plane heading south...

DEVILS & DEMONS: PART 2, $15.00 & $5.00 S/H: The Game is bitter-sweet for Talton, aka Gangsta. The same West Coast Clique who came to his aid ended up putting bullets into the chest of the woman he had fallen in love with. After leaving his ride or die in a puddle of her own blood, Talton finds himself on a flight back to Oak Park, the neighborhood where it all started...

The is the second installment of the Devils & Demons series. Once again, publishing boss Mike Enemigo and street-lit legend and screenwriter Kwame "Dutch" Teague have collaborated with The Cell Block's very own hitmaker, King Guru, to bring you this urban saga that promises to have you turning pages till your fingers bleed!

DEVILS & DEMONS: PART 3, $15.00 & $5.00 S/H: Talton is on the road to retribution for the murder of the love of his life. Dante and his crew of killers are on a

path of no return. This urban classic is based on real-life West Coast underworld politics. See what happens when a group of YG's find themselves in the midst of real underworld demons...
This is the third installment of the Devils & Demons series. Once again, publishing boss Mike Enemigo and street-lit legend and screenwriter Kwame "Dutch" Teague have collaborated with The Cell Block's very own hitmaker, King Guru, to bring you this urban saga that promises to have you turning pages till your fingers bleed!

DEVILS & DEMONS: PART 4, $15.00 & $5.00 S/H: After waking up from a coma, Alize has locked herself away from the rest of the world. When her sister Brittany and their friend finally take her on a girl's night out, she meets Luck – a drug dealing womanizer.

Things get complicated when the Columbian sisters who were with B.A. when he killed Mike in the first book of this series slide into the picture; it triggers a psychotic breakdown in the murderess known as Ze. Follow your favorite Devil as she explodes in her unpredictable actions of rage!

This is the fourth book in the Devils & Demons series, but it can also be read as book two.

Once again, publishing boss Mike Enemigo and street lit legend and screenwriter Kwame "Dutch" Teague have collaborated with The Cell Block's very own hitmaker, King Guru, to bring you this urban saga that promises to have you turning pages till your fingers bleed!

THE MILLIONAIRE PRISON: PART 3

THE ART & POWER OF LETTER WRITING FOR PRISONERS: DELUXE EDITION $19.99 & $7.00 S/H: When locked inside a prison cell, being able to write well is the most powerful skill you can have! Learn how to increase your power by writing high-quality personal and formal letters! Includes letter templates, pen-pal website strategies, punctuation guide and more!

THE PRISON MANUAL: $24.99 & $7.00 S/H: The Prison Manual is your all-in-one book on how to not only survive the rough terrain of the American prison system, but use it to your advantage so you can THRIVE from it! How to Use Your Prison Time to YOUR Advantage; How to Write Letters that Will Give You Maximum Effectiveness; Workout and Physical Health Secrets that Will Keep You as FIT as Possible; The Psychological impact of incarceration and How to Maintain Your MAXIMUM Level of Mental Health; Prison Art Techniques; Fulfilling Food Recipes; Parole Preparation Strategies and much, MUCH more!

GET OUT, STAY OUT!, $16.95 & $5.00 S/H: This book should be in the hands of everyone in a prison cell. It reveals a challenging but clear course for overcoming the obstacles that stand between prisoners and their freedom. For those behind bars, one goal outshines all others: GETTING OUT! After being released, that goal then shifts to STAYING OUT! This book will help prisoners do both. It has been masterfully constructed into five parts that will help prisoners maximize focus while they strive to accomplish whichever goal is at hand.

MOB$TAR MONEY, $12.00 & $4.00 S/H: After Trey's mother is sent to prison for 75 years to life, he and his little brother are moved from their home in Sacramento, California, to his grandmother's house in Stockton, California where he is forced to find his way in life and become a man on his own in the city's grimy streets. One day, on his way home from the local corner store, Trey has a rough encounter with the neighborhood bully. Luckily, that's when Tyson, a member of the MOBTAR, a local "get money" gang comes to his aid. The two kids quickly become friends, and it doesn't take long before Trey is embraced into the notorious MOB$TAR money gang, which opens the door to an adventure full of sex, money, murder and mayhem that will change his life forever... You will never guess how this story ends!

BLOCK MONEY, $12.00 & $4.00 S/H: Beast, a young thug from the grimy streets of central Stockton, California lives The Block; breathes The Block; and has committed himself to bleed The Block for all it's worth until his very last breath. Then, one day, he meets Nadia; a stripper at the local club who piques his curiosity with her beauty, quick-witted intellect and rider qualities. The problem? She has a man – Esco – a local kingpin with money and power. It doesn't take long, however, before a devious plot is hatched to pull off a heist worth an indeterminable amount of money. Following the acts of treachery, deception and betrayal are twists and turns and a bloody war that will leave you speechless!

HOW TO HUSTLE AND WIN: SEX, MONEY, MURDER EDITION $15.00 & $5.00 S/H: How To

THE MILLIONAIRE PRISON: PART 3

Hu$tle and Win: Sex, Money, Murder edition is the grittiest, underground self-help manual for the 21st century street entrepreneur in print. Never has there been such a book written for today's gangsters, goons and go-getters. This self-help handbook is an absolute must-have for anyone who is actively connected to the streets.

RAW LAW: Your Rights, & How to Sue When They are Violated! $15.00 & $5.00 S/H: Raw Law For Prisoners is a clear and concise guide for prisoners and their advocates to understanding civil rights laws guaranteed to prisoners under the US Constitution, and how to successfully file a lawsuit when those rights have been violated! From initial complaint to trial, this book will take you through the entire process, step by step, in simple, easy-to-understand terms. Also included are several examples where prisoners have sued prison officials successfully, resulting in changes of unjust rules and regulations and recourse for rights violations, oftentimes resulting in rewards of thousands, even millions of dollars in damages! If you feel your rights have been violated, don't lash out at guards, which is usually ineffective and only makes matters worse. Instead, defend yourself successfully by using the legal system, and getting the power of the courts on your side!

HOW TO WRITE URBAN BOOKS FOR MONEY & FAME: $16.95 & $5.00 S/H: Inside this book you will learn the true story of how Mike Enemigo and King Guru have received money and fame from inside their prison cells by writing urban books; the secrets to writing hood classics so you, too, can be caked up and famous; proper punctuation using hood examples; and resources you can use to achieve your money motivated ambitions! If you're a prisoner who want to write urban novels for money and fame, this must-have manual will give you all the game!

PRETTY GIRLS LOVE BAD BOYS: An Inmate's Guide to Getting Girls: $15.00 & $5.00 S/H: Tired of the same, boring, cliché pen pal books that don't tell you what you really need to know? If so, this book is for you! Anything you need to know on the art of long and short distance seduction is included within these pages! Not only does it give you the science of attracting pen pals from websites, it also includes psychological profiles and instructions on how to seduce any woman you set your sights on! Includes interviews of women who have fallen in love with prisoners, bios for pen pal ads, pre-written love letters, romantic poems, love-song lyrics, jokes and much, much more! This book is the ultimate guide – a must-have for any prisoner who refuses to let prison walls affect their MAC'n.

THE LADIES WHO LOVE PRISONERS, $15.00 & $5.00 S/H: New Special Report reveals the secrets of real women who have fallen in love with prisoners, regardless of crime, sentence, or location. This info will give you a HUGE advantage in getting girls from prison.

GET OUT, GET RICH: HOW TO GET PAID LEGALLY WHEN YOU GET OUT OF PRISON!, $16.95 & $5.00 S/H: Many of you are incarcerated for a money-motivated crime. But w/ today's tech & opportunities, not only is the crime-for-money risk/reward ratio not strategically wise, it's not even

THE MILLIONAIRE PRISON: PART 3

necessary. You can earn much more money by partaking in anyone of the easy, legal hustles explained in this book, regardless of your record. Help yourself earn an honest income so you can not only make a lot of money, but say good-bye to penitentiary chances and prison forever! (Note: Many things in this book can even he done from inside prison.) (ALSO PUBLISHED AS HOOD MILLIONAIRE: HOW TO HUSTLE AND WIN LEGALLY!)

THE MILLIONAIRE PRISONER: SPECIAL 2-IN-1 EDITION, $24.99 & $7.00 S/H: Why wait until you get out of prison to achieve your dreams? Here's a blueprint that you can use to become successful! The Millionaire Prisoner is your complete reference to overcoming any obstacle in prison. You won't be able to put it down! With this book you will discover the secrets to: Making money from your cell! Obtain FREE money for correspondence courses! Become an expert on any topic! Develop the habits of the rich! Network with celebrities! Set up your own website! Market your products, ideas and services! Successfully use prison pen pal websites! All of this and much, much more! This book has enabled thousands of prisoners to succeed and it will show you the way also!

THE MILLIONAIRE PRISONER 3: SUCCESS UNIVERSITY, $16.95 & $5 S/H: Why wait until you get out of prison to achieve your dreams? Here's a new-look blueprint that you can use to be successful! The Millionaire Prisoner 3 contains advanced strategies to overcoming any obstacle in prison. You won't be able to put it down!

THE CEO MANUAL: HOW TO START A BUSINESS WHEN YOU GET OUT OF PRISON, $16.95 & $5.00 S/H: $16.95 & $5 S/H: This new book will teach you the simplest way to start your own business when you get out of prison. Includes: Start-up Steps! The Secrets to Pulling Money from Investors! How to Manage People Effectively! How To Legally Protect Your Assets from "them"! Hundreds of resources to get you started, including a list of 'loan friendly" banks! (ALSO PUBLISHED AS CEO MANUAL: START A BUSINESS, BE A BOSS!)

THE MONEY MANUAL: UNDERGROUND CASH SECRETS EXPOSED! 16.95 & $5.00 S/H: Becoming a millionaire is equal parts what you make, and what you don't spend-- AKA save. All Millionaires and Billionaires have mastered the art of not only making money, but keeping the money they make (remember Donald Trump's tax maneuvers?), as well as establishing credit so that they are loaned money by banks and trusted with money from investors: AKA OPM -- other people's money. And did you know there are millionaires and billionaires just waiting to GIVE money away? It's true! These are all very-little known secrets 'they" don't want YOU to know about, but that I'm exposing in my new book!

OJ'S LIFE BEHIND BARS, $15.00 & $5 S/H: In 1994, Heisman Trophy winner and NFL superstar OJ Simpson was arrested for the brutal murder of his ex-wife Nicole Brown-Simpson and her friend Ron Goldman. In 1995, after the "trial of the century," he was acquitted of both murders, though most of the world believes he did it. In 2007 OJ was again arrested, but this time in Las Vegas, for armed robbery and kidnapping. On October 3, 2008 he was found guilty sentenced to 33 years and was sent to Lovelock Correctional Facility, in Lovelock, Nevada. There he met inmate-author Vernon Nelson. Vernon was granted a true, insider's perspective into the mind and life of one of the country's most notorious men; one that has never provided...until now.

BMF, $18.99 & $5 S/H: The Black Mafia Family was a drug organization headed by brothers Demetrius "Big Meech" Flenory and Terry "Southwest T" Flenory. Rising up from the shadows of Detroit's underbelly, they created a cross-country cocaine network, becoming two of the wealthiest, most dangerously sophisticated drug traffickers the United States has ever seen.

BLACK DYNASTY, $15.00 & $5 S/H: After their parents are murdered in cold blood, the Black siblings are left to fend for themselves in the unforgiving streets. But when the oldest brother, Lorenzo, is introduced to his deceased father's drug connection, he is given the opportunity of a lifetime to put his family back on top.

JAILHOUSE PUBLISHING For Money, Power & Fame: $24.99 & $7 S/H: In 2010, after flirting with the idea for two years, Mike Enemigo started writing his first book. In 2014, he officially launched his publishing company, The Cell Block, with the release of five books. Of course, with no mentor(s), how-to guides, or any real resources, he was met with failure after failure as he tried to navigate the treacherous goal of publishing books from his prison cell. However, he was determined to make it. He was determined to figure it out and he refused to quit. In Mike's new book, Jailhouse Publishing for Money, Power, and Fame, he breaks down all his jailhouse publishing secrets and strategies, so you can do all he's done, but without the trials and tribulations he's had to go through...

KITTY KAT, ADULT ENTERTAINMENT RESOURCE BOOK, $24.99 & $7.00 S/H: This book is jam packed with hundreds of sexy non nude photos including photo spreads. The book contains the complete info on sexy photo sellers, hot magazines, page turning bookstore, sections on strip clubs, porn stars, alluring models, thought provoking stories and must-see movies.

PRISON LEGAL GUIDE, $24.99 & $7.00 S/H: The laws of the U.S. Judicial system are complex, complicated, and always growing and changing. Many prisoners spend days on end digging through its intricacies. Pile on top of the legal code the rules and regulations of a correctional facility, and you can see how high the deck is being stacked against you. Correct legal information is the key to your survival when you have run afoul of the system (or it is running afoul of you). Whether you are an accomplished jailhouse lawyer helping newbies learn the ropes, an old head fighting bare-knuckle for your rights in the courts, or a hustler just looking to beat the latest write-up – this book has something for you!

PRISON HEALTH HANDBOOK, $19.99 & $7.00 S/H: The Prison Health Handbook is your one-stop go-

THE MILLIONAIRE PRISON: PART 3

to source for information on how to maintain your best health while inside the American prison system. Filled with information, tips, and secrets from doctors, gurus, and other experts, this book will educate you on such things as proper workout and exercise regimens; yoga benefits for prisoners; how to meditate effectively; pain management tips; sensible dieting solutions; nutritional knowledge; an understanding of various cancers, diabetes, hepatitis, and other diseases all too common in prison; how to effectively deal with mental health issues such as stress, PTSD, anxiety, and depression; a list of things your doctors DON'T want YOU to know; and much, much more!

All books are available on Amazon and thecellblock.net website. Prices may differ between Amazon and our website.

You can also order by sending a money order or institutional check to:

The Cell Block
PO Box 1025
Rancho Cordova, CA 95741

www.ingramcontent.com/pod-product-compliance
Lightning Source LLC
Chambersburg PA
CBHW050858160426
43194CB00011B/2198